# Teen Miracles

## Extraordinary life-changing stories
## from today's teens

Marsha Arons

ADAMS MEDIA
Avon, Massachusetts

Published by
Adams Media, an F+W Publications Company
57 Littlefield Street, Avon, MA 02322. U.S.A.
*www.adamsmedia.com*

ISBN: 1-58062-758-7

Printed in Canada.

J I H G F E D C B A

**Library of Congress Cataloging-in-Publication Data**
Arons, Marsha.
Teen miracles / Marsha Arons.
p.    cm.
Summary: A collection of stories about teenagers who
feel that some power greater than themselves has
orchestrated miraculous events in their lives.
ISBN 1-58062-758-7
1. Miracles. 2. Teenagers--United States. [1. Miracles.] I. Title.
BL487.A76        2004
204'.32--dc22    2003017009

This publication is designed to provide accurate and authoritative information with regard to the subject matter covered. It is sold with the understanding that the publisher is not engaged in rendering legal, accounting, or other professional advice. If legal advice or other expert assistance is required, the services of a competent professional person should be sought.
—From a *Declaration of Principles* jointly adopted by a Committee of the American Bar Association and a Committee of Publishers and Associations

Many of the designations used by manufacturers and sellers to distinguish their products are claimed as trademarks. Where those designations appear in this book and Adams Media was aware of a trademark claim, the designations have been printed with initial capital letters.

While all the events and experiences recounted in this book are inspired by real people, some of the names, dates, and places have been changed in order to protect the privacy of certain individuals.

*This book is available at quantity discounts for bulk purchases.*
*For information, call 1-800-872-5627*

# Permissions

"Real Life Angel," page 233, by Rebecca Steinberg, reprinted by permission.

"Déjà vu," page 174, by Marina Traskunova, reprinted by permission.

"Seeing Is Believing," page 229, by Jason Leib, reprinted by permission.

"Miracle Mom," page 143, by Danielle Gershon, reprinted by permission.

"Exactly Right," page 224; "Joanne," page 238; "Riding in Cars," page 218; "Chance Encounter," page 119; and "Inner Resources," page 167, by Phyllis Nutkis, reprinted by permission.

"Yvette," page 199, by Nikki Kohlenbrener, reprinted by permission.

# Acknowledgments

Special thanks to Phyllis Nutkis, writer, teacher, therapist, and friend extraordinaire. Phyllis listens with her heart and hears the stories of children of all ages. Her help and support in creating this manuscript were invaluable.

Thank you also to Shayna Gould, Jason Leib, Marina Traskunova, Mark Dalton, Tameka Brown, Maracita Xavier, Steven Ninn, Nikki Kohlenbrener, Danielle Gershon, Rebecca Steinberg, Mary Margaret O'Casey, Tina Beaufort, Emmet Cardoza, John Jamison, and all the other teens whose personal experiences inspired these stories. Your ideas, suggestions, and unique teen perspective on life, faith, and hope make me glad that I chose the profession I did. You all make me realize that we all have reason to believe in miracles.

To Norman Nutkis, director of guidance, Milwaukee Public Schools; Dale Dresdner, special education and learning disabilities teacher; and all the other educators who allowed me into their classrooms and schools and who offered me help and guidance with this book, my heartfelt gratitude.

To Gayle Kopin, gifted English teacher of my own children, who took great pains with this manuscript and offered so many wonderful suggestions.

This book is dedicated to my wonderful husband Rick, who shows his faith in God and in my abilities daily, and to my beautiful daughters, Anna, Rachael, Kayla, and Elliana, who let me know by their very presence that God is truly good.

# Introduction

*I*n doing research for this book, I spoke to teens from many different venues and in many different circumstances. And what I learned in doing these interviews assured me that, if these young people are our future, we have good reason to have hope for a better world. These teens struggle with the same questions that have defined the human condition for centuries: Am I good enough? Will I succeed? What is my place? My role? How can I find happiness? But I also heard some other questions from these teenagers: How can I make a difference in someone else's life? How can I change things and make them better? Am I part of a bigger plan?

The answers came from the teenagers themselves. They told stories that showed both them and me that when they were called on, they often responded with their best selves, evidencing courage, fortitude, and a strength of character that even they themselves may not have realized they possessed.

These teenagers felt part of a set of miraculous events, orchestrated by some power greater than themselves. They—and I—found comfort in this feeling. To feel blessed, taken care of, watched over is a wonderful thing. It gives us hope and encourages us to reach into ourselves and bring out those best instincts that enable us to rise to others' highest expectations of us.

These stories are inspirational not just for the power of the experiences themselves but for the effect they have on each of us as we identify with the speaker. And we do identify with them.

What unites us all—and these stories—is what defines us as human beings who care for and about one another. It is that wonderful thing that allows us to accept the help we may need in fulfilling our destinies.

It is the belief in miracles.

We all need to believe in our own abilities, our own power to accomplish miracles, to have a positive effect on the world.

Miracles come to us in many ways. When we open our hearts and minds, they come to us, whispering their presence or screaming to get our attention. They never leave us untouched. They offer us the comfort of knowing that, in a world where there is pain and suffering, faith and hope also exist.

The stories themselves convey this message. But I found that the storytellers themselves communicated this as well. These young adults showed me the best that we have to offer: courage, strength of character, compassion, ability to love in abundance—all the ingredients that we need to make the world a better place. And that is perhaps the most exciting miracle of all.

This book is for every teen who has ever been part of a miracle, and for every teen who has ever needed one.

—Marsha Arons
Skokie, IL
May 2003

My sister, Jodie, and I are identical twins. Most people meeting us for the first time have trouble telling us apart. Our close friends don't have this difficulty though, because my sister and I have very different personalities. We have different tastes in clothes, in music, and especially in boys. This is probably a good thing because we don't have to compete with each other. We also both have tempers, and if we were to argue over some boy . . . well, let's just say, things could get ugly.

Even though we are so different, we really enjoy spending time together. I think Jodie is the funniest, smartest person I know. She's really my best friend because, when you get right down to it, you can always count on your sister to be there when you need her. Of course, since we share a room, there are plenty of times when my sister is there even when I don't need her!

People always want to know if it is true that twins have a special language all their own. My mother says that we didn't talk very early because, as babies, we made noises that only we understood and that seemed to be enough for us until we were about a year and a half. I don't know if we have a special language, but one thing I do know: We have a unique way of communicating that no one else has. This story is a case in point.

Our parents had left us at home for a weekend. My father often travels on business, and this time, he was going someplace fun, so my mother decided to accompany him. We were sixteen, old enough to be responsible, my mother said, so she wasn't going to ask Mrs. James down the street to stay with us. (Thank God she decided that. My friends would have laughed themselves sick to think that Jodie and I had to have a babysitter at our age!) But because my mother is still the overprotective type, she did arrange for Mrs. James to "look in on us," particularly at night to make sure that we had locked up properly.

That was okay with Jodie and me. Mrs. James is really a lot cooler than my parents know. When we were little, she used to baby-sit for us, and she took us out for ice cream a lot more often than my parents would have liked. And once when I was about fourteen, I went to a party while my parents were away and Mrs. James was babysitting. I came home an hour later than curfew, but Mrs. James never told my parents. I did cut her lawn and water her plants for a month after that, but that arrangement was just between Mrs. James and me.

Anyway, on Friday afternoon after school, Jodie announced that she was going to the mall to get to a sale at Glenda's. She asked me if I wanted to come. Glenda's is one of our favorite stores. It's kind of trendy, but the clothes are well made. Usually, if Jodie buys something there, I end up borrowing it. We share a lot of our clothes though sometimes we fight about it.

But it was a beautiful day out, and I decided to go rollerblading instead. "Pick up something I'll like, too," I told her. "See you later."

It was a beautiful day out, just a little cool for May. I didn't care. I pulled on one of my favorite big fleecy pullover sweaters and went to find my rollerblades.

Now, that sweater is one item of clothing I don't like to share with Jodie. It is very special to me for sentimental reasons. It is a funny purple color and has a big star in the middle of it. My friend Nancy gave it to me when I was Dorothy in our eighth-grade production of *The Wizard of Oz,* to remind me that I'd always be a star to her. Her family moved away a short time after that, and I missed her a lot.

Because the sweater was so thick and fleecy, I didn't bother to put on my wrist guards. They bother me if I put them under the sweater, and they don't fit over the sleeves of it. I figured if I fell, my arms would be protected. So I just strapped on my shin guards and my helmet and went to get my rollerblades.

And tripped over them! I had left them at the bottom of the basement steps, and in the dim light, I didn't see them. I fell headfirst across the cement floor of the basement, putting my arms out to catch myself.

I knew my arm was broken without even being able to see it under my long sleeve. The pain was so intense, I couldn't help screaming. But then I realized that there was no one home to hear me. For a minute, my stomach dropped in real panic as

I fought to remain rational. The telephone! I had to reach the phone! Then, as if by magic, the phone started to ring. Only, I couldn't reach it. The pain when I moved made me so sick to my stomach that I stopped trying. That was when panic gave way to horrific pain, and I stayed where I was.

But suddenly, I heard a voice above me, calling me, "Jennifer?" It was Mrs. James. I didn't know why she had chosen that moment to check on us, but I was so happy she was there, I cried. Well, I cried for a lot of reasons.

"Down here! Help me!" I called. She didn't try to move me. But she dialed 911 on the cell phone in her hand.

The last thing I saw before I drifted mercifully into sleep was the scissors as the nurse prepared to cut away the arm of my favorite sweater so that the doctors could set my badly broken arm.

When I woke up, Jodie and Mrs. James were next to me, and my arm was in a cast up to my shoulder. The pain wasn't terrible; Jodie informed me that I had been given painkillers. Then she grinned as she held up the doctor's prescription for additional painkillers. "Mom and Dad aren't going to like that I let you get into drugs while they were gone!" she joked.

Both bones in my arm were broken—right through the skin. "It's a good thing you were wearing something over your arms so you didn't have to see it!" said Jodie.

Oh, my favorite sweater! I remembered. They cut it off me. I realized I was wearing a hospital gown. I looked at Mrs. James. Her worried expression made me smile at her. "Don't worry," I told her. "I'll be okay. And thanks for coming over to check on me! I don't know what I would have done if you hadn't come then."

Even as I said it, I saw Jodie and Mrs. James exchange glances. Then Mrs. James said, "You can thank your twin sister here for that. I was determined not to interfere with you girls. I was only going to come over in the evenings as I promised your mother. But Jodie called and asked me to go over then. She was so insistent that I hurried right over!"

I looked at my sister. "How did you know? What made you call Mrs. James?" I asked. She was quiet for a minute. Then she said, "Look Jennifer, I was at Glenda's and I saw a great sweater. It was perfect for you and just as I picked it up to look at the size, I got the strangest sensation. I called you from the mall. But there was no answer. I tried to tell myself that I was imagining things, that I shouldn't bother Mrs. James. But when I was at the cash register paying for the sweater and the clerk gave it to me—that's when I felt it the strongest. I figured Mrs. James wouldn't mind just one extra little visit to our house!"

Other people would never believe it. They wouldn't understand how twins could be so in sync with one another that they could feel when one was in trouble. But Jodie and I knew. And we weren't too surprised.

At least we weren't too surprised until later at home, when Mrs. James had had dinner with us and gone to fill my prescription. Then I opened the package that my sister had bought for me at Glenda's. There, inside the box, was indeed the perfect sweater for me. It was just like the one I had been wearing when I fell, the one the nurse had destroyed when they set my arm. The sweater was purple fleece with a big white star on the front. Only, this one was button-down, so I could wear it over my huge cast.

This sweater means so much more to me than the other one did. But this one, I think I'll let my sister borrow! ✳

*I*'ve played basketball since the fifth grade. My friends and I play on the girl's high school team, and we have a pretty good record. I play forward mostly. Sometimes I'm the guard, though. I do all right under the boards but I have no outside shot.

We usually draw a big crowd, which is really gratifying because women's basketball in our area has always kind of taken a back seat. The boy's team has always gotten a lot of attention, and it's really thrilling to look up into the stands and see all those fans (and not just our parents and friends) cheering for us.

I love everything about the game—the feeling of being part of a team, wearing the uniform, and running out on the court to the cheers and screams of the crowd. I love the drive to the basket and the run downcourt to catch the hard pass and put it up. And, of course, there's that sweet, sweet moment when the ball leaves your hands at just the right angle, with just the right force, and you know your aim is true. Then, the announcer says your name over the loudspeaker with just that perfect inflection, and you know you've made your friends and family proud. You can almost feel their joy with your whole body as you turn to set up your defense for the next play.

My grandfather has come to see me play ever since I was little. He loves the sport, and we've gone to many professional games together. He's always told me that women can play basketball as well as any man, and the secret to success is concentration and practice. I'm very close to him, and I know he's proud of me even when we lose, if he knows I've done my best. It's not possible to disappoint him; he loves me so much!

This past season was rocky for us from the start. We played some new teams that joined our league, and we had to adjust our strategy to beat them. But we have a great coach, and he's terrific at assessing the opposition. He has an uncanny knack for being able to spot their strengths and weaknesses.

Our season picked up in the middle and we had a hot streak. As we neared the championship game, we knew we had a chance to take it all. The quarter finals were easy. We won by twenty points. But the next round was harder. The other team was clearly as good as ours, so we just fought it out. We won that game by a few points.

It really psyched us up for the championship game. It was scheduled for a Sunday afternoon to allow as many people as possible to attend. For two solid weeks, all conversation with my friends centered on the upcoming game. All of my free time was spent practicing. Studying wasn't my first priority. I didn't care though. If we won that championship, we would be the first women's team in the history of our school to do it, and I wanted that trophy.

One week before the big game, my grandfather had a mild heart attack. I say "mild" because he didn't pass out. He was eating dinner at our house and thought he was having indigestion. I was about to make a wisecrack about my mother's cooking when Granddad got a peculiar look on his face. My mom drove him to the hospital. In retrospect, I suppose we should have called an ambulance. That's what you're supposed to do. But he didn't seem that sick and he could still talk to us. But when he winced while I helped him on with his coat, I felt a sudden stab of fear. But Granddad hugged me and told me not to worry; he would see me soon.

He was right. He was out of the hospital in three days. The doctors told us we were lucky. It was a warning, they said. He needed surgery to clear a blocked artery, and they scheduled him for the Friday after my game. I think my grandfather felt more inconvenienced than anything else. The list of foods he couldn't have because of the salt content included many of his favorites, and he knew he'd have to make a lot of lifestyle changes. I told him I'd take walks with him.

I was so relieved when I found out he was okay. I desperately wanted him to be there for my big game. My parents would come, of course, and my brother. But it was Granddad who made me give that extra push when I played. And I wanted to win so badly! I think it was always in the back of my mind somewhere—that selfish fear that maybe he wouldn't be able to see me play. I was too ashamed to say anything, but, as usual, he knew what I was thinking. When he came home, the first thing he said to me was, "You don't think I'd miss the chance to see my favorite basketball star win the game, do you?"

We really did play well. But the other team played well, too. It was a battle all the way. It came down to less than a minute on the clock. We were down by two. Just one more basket, I prayed silently. Then we could go into overtime. But there were so many turnovers during that last minute.

They had possession and were under our basket. Suddenly, I saw my chance. I slapped the ball out of the shooter's hands. It was a clean steal, no foul! The guard snatched it up as I started my run downcourt. The crowd was on its feet counting down the clock. That ball sailed right into my hands on the pass and I looked toward the basket. I was only at mid-court.

What happened next was in slow motion, it seemed. I had never had a good outside shot and there was no way in the world I could sink a shot from the half-court line. But something made me throw that ball hard. If I live to be 100, I will never forget that feeling. I knew it when the ball left my hands with all the force I had within me. I knew it when that ball arched perfectly, finding the basket cleanly just at the buzzer! The perfect shot! And a three-pointer!

The crowd swooped down on us, screaming and cheering. Someone passed me the trophy and I held it high above my head for all to see. I caught sight of my grandfather in the stands. He was on his feet and his grin was so wide, I could see every tooth in his mouth from the court. He nodded his head at me in that special way he had, and I knew what he was feeling. My grandfather would have been proud of me, even if we hadn't won. I had played my best. But, this! A three-pointer! Who would ever have believed it possible?

My grandfather died peacefully in his sleep four days later. At the funeral, I didn't cry. I knew I had witnessed a true miracle. My grandfather lived to see me accomplish something I had dreamed of. I had the most amazing sense that my grandfather knew his time was up and he wasn't afraid to go. The night he had his "warning" at dinner wasn't his time. He had unfinished business. He had to see me win that game.

No, I didn't cry then, though I am crying now as I write this four months later. I miss him. I always will. But I know, without any doubt at all, that wherever Granddad is now, he's with me, just like always. He'll be there next year, cheering me on as I play for the college team.

Sometimes when I'm playing in a pickup game, I feel his presence so strongly that, before I can catch myself, I look around for his face.

That three-pointer was guided by unseen hands, hands that had the power to perform a miracle just for my grandfather and me, hands that didn't snatch him away from us before he had the chance to see me do the unbelievable, hands that are holding Granddad now. Those are some powerful hands!

I wonder if God plays basketball. *

*As part of my scholarship package* when I began my freshman year at a New York university, I got a job in a hospital on the Upper West Side of Manhattan. Since I was a biology major and thinking about going into medicine, I was really excited about working there even though I was sure that the work I would be given wouldn't be anything very important or exciting—probably filing or taking flowers to patients. I was wrong.

I was assigned to the Neonatal (newborn) Intensive Care Unit as part of a special program. The hospital labor and delivery department attracts a large number of mothers who use drugs, and often their babies are born early and with drugs, particularly crack cocaine, in their system. These babies require special care and a great deal of hands-on contact, something the nurses and doctors are often too overworked to give. College students like me get paid essentially to hold these babies and try to give them some comfort during their first weeks of life. Often these babies are not expected to go home with their own mothers but will be sent into foster care. Many of the babies don't go home at all.

On some days, I worked from five to ten in the evening. Other days, I worked from seven in the morning to twelve noon. I was rarely asked to work other hours than my usual shift.

It shocked me the first time I saw a newborn die. She was a little under four pounds at birth and when I saw her she was hooked up to all kinds of tubes. Even so she was a funny bluish color and she twitched. But she never cried. Her silence bothered me more than anything else about her. Somehow I felt it just wasn't right that this little girl never even got to have a say about anything in her brief life. She never got to cry out in protest at the mother who loved her drugs better than she loved her own baby. I was there when this baby died, though I never got to touch or hold her. The doctor who disconnected all her tubes sighed, then called the time of death. I saw her pass her hand over her eyes in a tired way as if she had done this many times before. When I asked her how many times this had happened since she started working at the hospital, she said, "Too many."

The first time I saw a doctor administer to the baby the same kind of drug that his mother had been addicted to, I was shocked! Then it was explained to me how it was a slightly different drug, but that the baby had to be weaned off all drugs slowly. Withdrawal is a gradual process, and painful. But for some of these babies, the treatment they received at least gave them a fighting chance.

I had been working at the hospital for about six months when a young woman gave birth to a little boy who tested positive for cocaine. I never got to see the mother. If she made any attempt to see her son, I never saw it. In fact, I never saw any relative come to see this little boy.

I was assigned to hold this little boy each day that I came to the hospital. I held him, walked him, rocked him and sang to him, always mindful of the tubes that ran in and out of his little body. My work took on a routine. I would punch the time clock; wash up; gown, glove, and mask myself and then find little Pedro. (That was the name the nurses had given him. The nurses named all the babies because it made them seem like people; it gave them a little dignity.)

At first, Pedro was just like all the other babies, same bluish kind of color, attached to a bunch of tubes. But Pedro had been born weighing over five pounds, a lot for a cocaine baby. The doctors thought he had a good chance. So did I. Maybe that was why I allowed myself to feel close to this baby. The staff had warned me not to let this happen.

But Pedro was different from the other babies. He really opened his eyes and looked directly into mine when I held him. He still twitched and cried fretfully, but he seemed to respond a lot when I held him. He especially liked to hear me sing!

I sang whatever I could think of. I even sang him the Yiddish and German lullabies my grandmother used to sing to me when I was a little girl.

As the days passed, I noticed that he seemed a little brighter, more responsive. He gained a little weight. But when I told Nurse Holland that I thought Pedro was doing better, she said, "Rachael, don't get too attached. Pedro has a hole in his heart and he will need surgery to fix it. Unless someone—his family or the state—pays for it, it is likely that he will die before he can have it."

I didn't want to believe it. I turned away so the nurse wouldn't see the tears in my eyes.

One day, I stayed with Pedro an extra-long time, singing and stroking him as usual. He slept peacefully as long as I continued to touch him. If I took my hand away, he roused uncomfortably. The same thing happened if I stopped singing.

All the doctors and nurses at that hospital kept warning me that I was bound to get my heart broken, that Pedro, like many other babies, would die. I had to do something! But what?

On the subway ride back to my dorm, it came to me! I suddenly remembered an old custom my grandmother told me about, a superstition about changing the name of a sick person. If someone was so sick that they might die, the family changed his name in order to fool the angel of death. "He's not so smart," said my grandmother. "If he comes for Joe and finds only David, then off he goes, leaving David alone!"

The next day in the hospital when I picked up Pedro, I said, "Hello, David! How are you feeling today?" Even when I wasn't holding him but just passing his bassinet, I'd look at him and say, "Hi, David!"

The nursing staff began calling him David, too, never even asking me why. As I left one Thursday afternoon, I said goodbye to David and told him that I'd see him on my shift at five the following day. I had a big English test to study for, so I needed to get to the library. I knew I was headed for an all-nighter.

I was right. I studied until three; then I crept back to my dorm for a few hours of sleep before my test at ten.

When the phone rang at five A.M., it sounded like cannon fire. I groped for it sleepily, silently cursing anyone who had the nerve to call at that hour. But the speaker's words made me instantly awake.

"Hello, Rachael, this is Miss Peabody on the graveyard shift at the hospital. Could you please come right over? We've had a rash of new babies during the night, and we are extremely shorthanded. Your special friend has been very restless, too." I didn't know Miss Peabody, probably because I'd never worked the hours from midnight until six in the morning, but when she mentioned David, I told her I'd be right there.

It was my usual routine, or so I thought. I punched in at 5:44 A.M. washed and gowned. The nursery was hopping—there were several new babies being evaluated and attended by the nursing staff. I went over to David's bassinet. I noticed that there was a white blanket in the crib and a breathing tube next to him. It was odd to see that tube lying there like that. But maybe a doctor had placed it where it could be reached easily in case David needed it. But David's breathing seemed to be fine. In fact, David seemed to weigh more, too, when I picked him up. I began to sing to him.

When the nursery finally settled down, I was sitting in the rocking chair. To my surprise, three nurses looked at me at once and covered their mouths with their hands!

Then the resident caught sight of me. He gasped and cried, "What on earth are you doing?" I was so shocked, I could only stammer, "Why . . . I'm holding David . . . just like I always do! What's wrong?" The look on their faces terrified me.

The resident came over and looked at the baby. So did the nurses. David cooed a little at them. In another minute, the whole staff had gathered around me. What was going on?

The resident said, "This baby was dead! I called the code and then pronounced him. We worked on him for fifteen minutes but we couldn't restart his heart! Look, Rachael, see? Time of Death: 5:50 A.M."

Nobody said a word. Nobody could believe what they were seeing, not even me. I had clocked in six minutes before David "died"—six minutes! At 5:44 when I had picked him up, he was still alive. And he certainly was alive and kicking now!

They say all babies are miracles. But the one I was holding really gave new meaning to that term. The angel of death may have intended to take Pedro at 5:50 A.M. But that stupid angel had arrived to find David instead and so David had been left alive for me to find him at 5:44 A.M.

The staff bustled around all day, talking about it. How could such a thing happen in a big, major hospital like this one? The doctors and nurses were beside themselves. Nobody had ever heard of such a thing.

Nobody, as it turned out, had ever heard of Miss Peabody working the graveyard shift, either. ✳

*K*eisha and I have known each other since kindergarten. At that age, little girls form friendships based on what is really important, so even though Keisha is African-American and I am white, race has never been an issue between us. We have always respected one another. Over the years, the neighborhood we lived in changed a lot. My family moved out when I was in sixth grade. Keisha's family stayed. I went to a different middle school, and we kept in touch, but then we both went to the same high school.

Keisha was an average student. In our high school, there were other things that kids had to worry about besides just homework—things like getting home after school without getting shot at or hit on; things like getting your boyfriend to care whether or not you got pregnant. School was a place where everyone watched out for themselves.

But Keisha and I—we always watched out for each other. She taught me a phrase: "We always have each other's back." It meant that even in our most vulnerable spots, the places we couldn't see, situations we couldn't predict, we each had a friend to turn to when we needed one. In high school, there are all kinds of ways that people get hurt, emotionally and physically. Keisha and I were lucky to have each other and we both knew it.

At the beginning of our senior year, Keisha began to date a guy named Tyrese. He was beautiful; there was no doubt about that. And from what Keisha told me, he was really good to her. I was glad to hear it because the guys at our school were usually in a gang of some sort and they didn't treat their women very well. I got through my high school years pretty much avoiding these types, concentrating on getting good grades.

But Keisha lived in a different part of town and she personally knew most of the guys in the gangs. Tyrese was different. He was friends with a lot of groups but he didn't hang with any one of them. He had an after-school job that took up a lot of his free time.

I got to be friends with Tyrese because of Keisha. The two of them came to my house on the weekends. We listened to music, ate a lot, and just hung out.

Tyrese was really good with his hands. He liked to fix things. Once he fixed my mother's refrigerator. He had a hard time convincing my mother to let him try. But when she looked at the water running out on the floor and saw how everything inside was spoiling and was told that the repairman couldn't get there until Tuesday, she said okay.

"You've got nothing to lose." Tyrese grinned. He fixed it and my mother was happy she didn't have to pay a repairman. Tyrese wouldn't take any money, either. He said my mother fed him often enough.

So, we all grew to like Tyrese, and I was happy for Keisha.

At the beginning of December, things began to change for

all of us. It started with a phone call I got from Keisha.

"Jess, I'm scared!" Keisha said. I could tell she was crying. She was worried Tyrese was thinking about getting into a gang. "I know they've been after him," she said.

I knew what she was talking about. The kids at school— they don't let you alone. It was only a matter of time before they started looking for someone like Tyrese. In that world, you're either one of them or you're the enemy. I didn't know which was worse.

Tyrese was so close to graduating. He could get away from them after that. With his skills, my parents said, he was sure to find a job away from the neighborhood he lived in. My dad even offered to help him. If only he could hold out until June . . .

Now Keisha was telling me it didn't seem likely that Tyrese could avoid joining one of the gangs. And if he did join, he'd have to do something terrible—that's how they initiate you. I didn't know what to say to her.

I had applied to college and received my acceptance letter right after winter vacation. Keisha and Tyrese were happy for me even though it meant I'd be leaving town. We talked a little about plans for the future. It was clear that Keisha and Tyrese were thinking about being together. But I knew Keisha was scared for him. When I got Tyrese alone, I told him to be careful. We all had such hopes for the future! He just shrugged his shoulders.

Then he told me he was making something special for Keisha for Valentine's Day. He got really excited but he made me promise to keep it a secret. It was a nameplate, he said, forged out of iron. He was making it in Industrial Arts, his favorite class.

"I'm making one for her and one for me. We're gonna use it when we get jobs so people will know who we are. Don't you worry, Jess. Keisha and me—we're gonna make it out of here!" Tyrese sounded confident.

Two days later, Tyrese showed me the nameplates. They were beautiful—polished iron and brass with the letters in relief so you could read them easily. They were about four inches long and two inches wide. I could see them on a big, important door somewhere. I hoped both my friends would get to use them.

The day before Valentine's Day, Tyrese was especially edgy. When I asked him what was wrong, he didn't say. I thought he was excited about giving Keisha his gift. But when I look back, I should have seen that he wasn't happy and excited. He was scared and nervous.

Since the Columbine High School shootings, all public high schools in the city of Chicago have metal detectors. Ours are located just inside the front doors, and there is a guard who checks to make sure that no one has any weapons of any kind. Backpacks and purses are hand searched. We all know the routine.

Before I reached the front doors, Tyrese was by my side. "Here Jess, take these in for me, okay? I don't want Keisha to see them until after school."

He handed me the plates. Made of iron, they felt heavy in my hand. I arranged to meet Tyrese between third and fourth periods to give him back the plates. I showed them to the guard; then I put them in my backpack and went to class.

When it happened, it was so quick, I couldn't even remember all the details to tell the police. I saw Tyrese coming down the stairs as I was going up between classes. I was about to say, "Hey, Tyrese, let me give you the plates now," as I stepped in front of him looking up. But I never had the chance to get the words out of my mouth. He was looking down the stairs past me.

I saw his eyes go wide and heard him scream something like, "No! Man! Not here!" I heard a *pop!* Then suddenly I saw Tyrese take a flying leap over whoever was standing on the stairs between him and me. He landed on top of me, knocking me into the wall. I hit my head, hard.

There were a lot of screams and I didn't know what happened until some moments later. My head hurt, and Tyrese was still lying on top of me, breathing hard. He looked directly into my eyes.

Never have I ever seen such terror on anyone's face. "Jess! You all right?" Tyrese asked, standing up. He pulled me to my feet. I looked down to see Darren, a kid with a bad rep lying facedown on the floor. Two boys were sitting on top of him. In another minute the guards were there and Tyrese pulled me to the top of the stairwell. I watched from there as Darren was pulled to his feet, handcuffed, and led away. He screamed something disgusting. It took me a minute to realize he was aiming those words at Tyrese.

He had also aimed something else at Tyrese. One of the cops picked up a small handgun and put it into a bag. I sat down heavily on the stairwell landing, dazed.

From somewhere, Keisha appeared. She let out a shriek and pulled my backpack around. If I hadn't been sitting then, I would have fallen down. There in the middle of my backpack was a small-caliber bullet hole! I couldn't move. Tyrese reached into my bag and pulled out the plates. The *e* in Keisha's name had been pushed in so far, it made a bulge on the backside of the plate. The bullet was lying in the bottom of my bag.

The police put it all together. That bullet had been meant for Tyrese, but I stepped in front of him just as Darren fired. Tyrese had tried to protect me by knocking me down, but he was a fraction of a second too late. If I hadn't had the plates in my backpack, I would have been dead.

My friends are getting married right after graduation. Tyrese has a great job lined up working for a contractor. Keisha is starting college in the city.

It's nice to know that while I always had one close friend, I now have two who give new meaning to the term, "I've got your back!" ✳

*I* couldn't do anything right. For as long as I could remember, adults were always telling me to sit down and be quiet, to stop being disruptive, annoying, argumentative. I didn't mean to be that way; I just couldn't help it. I had trouble sitting still, not calling out the answer if I knew it (and sometimes even if I didn't), and concentrating on what people were saying to me.

School was torture even though I was pretty smart. I usually finished my work before the other kids, and I couldn't sit still, so I just had to walk around the room. The other kids complained that I was bothering them. My teachers sent me out of the classroom and I spent at least half of my school day in the hallway. Other kids would make fun of me.

One time my teacher got so mad at me that she made the other kids write letters to me telling me how they felt toward me. Maybe the teacher thought she could shame me into behaving. She shamed me all right.

My parents were always yelling at me for my bad behavior at home, too. They took me to a doctor, who said I had attention deficit disorder. He gave me medicine.

I really wanted to be good. I wanted the other kids to like me, and I wanted my parents to be proud of me. I got pretty good grades in school even though I wasn't in class a lot and couldn't seem to get my homework done. But if the subject was interesting to me, like math and science, I just read the text-book. When I took the test, I got an A.

But it didn't make my parents proud.

One summer, my parents found a Counselor-in-Training program for kids with ADD. They signed me up and I hoped I could get respect from doing a job well and I wouldn't be a total loser. But after a week, I got into a fight with another kid and the camp threw me out.

"What are we going to do with you, Sam?" my mother screamed. "Dad and I have to go to work and we can't just leave you home all day doing nothing. You'll find some trouble to get into." There I was—sixteen years old and my parents were afraid to let me stay home by myself.

My dad looked in the local park district catalogue and found a life-guarding course. It started the next day and ran for two weeks. I liked being in the water and I was a very good swimmer. I had even been on the swim team during my freshman and sophomore years of high school. He called and signed me up on the spot.

It turned out to be a pretty good thing. I found it was a lot easier to listen to the instructor and to follow directions given in the water instead of in the classroom. I passed with no trouble and got my lifeguard certification.

I also got a job! One of the lifeguards at the local beach wanted to take two weeks off, and my instructor asked me if I wanted the job. I almost jumped at the offer.

The first day I reported to work at the guard station and got my assignment. The beach is private, operated by the city. In the morning, the local day camps use the beach exclusively. I was assigned to guard the day campers in Sector B. I got my official whistle and rescue board. A rescue board is made of Styrofoam and shaped like a giant hot dog. If a guard has to make a rescue, he carries it with him on the run into the water. The board helps the guard keep his head out of the water so he can keep his victim in view.

I really understood lifesaving. I was proud of my knowledge and for the first time, I had confidence in my ability and I was going to hold on to this job. I liked the other guards and I would have some friends. And my parents would be proud of me.

The little kids' camp groups started arriving around nine-thirty. There were three of them, around 100 campers altogether, and each group was assigned to a particular sector with a particular guard. I got a group of eight-year-olds.

I first noticed the little boy because he was the only one without a buddy. He was hopping and dancing so much that his counselor asked him twice if he needed to go to the bathroom. He said no both times. As we walked out to the beach, he fell into step beside me.

His name was Andy and he asked me a million questions. What was my board for? What was it made of? How much did it weigh? Could he touch it? I answered all his questions and found that it was fun to be the teacher for a change. But when all the kids headed down to the water, Andy asked if he could climb up into my guard's chair with me. I had to say no; it was against the rules. And I couldn't keep talking to him because I had to keep my eyes and my mind on the water.

I saw Andy wander down to the water's edge and sit down next to a group of kids who were building something in the sand. He didn't join them—he just kind of played next to them, glancing up at them every now and then. I was too far away to hear if they spoke to him.

My heart turned over for this little guy.

Every day it was like that for him.

I felt so sorry for him. He was just like me! I wondered if he had ADD, too. He certainly seemed to have all the signs.

Toward the end of my second week on the job, the weather became unbearably hot. I was really glad for the heat wave, though. My supervisor told me that if the beaches were really crowded, they would keep me on even after the other lifeguard came back.

I was thinking about this while I was guarding the campers. Most of them were in the water since it was so hot!

I looked around for Andy. I noticed he was following some of the kids into the water. Then he started splashing them. I imagined they were telling him to stop because they seemed to splash back and moved away from him. I couldn't hear them but I could see them. He only wanted to play with them, I thought. Why couldn't they let him?

It was because I sympathized with Andy so much that I knew what was happening. He had indeed moved off from the other kids. But he moved farther out into the lake. He wasn't beyond the buoy that marked the swimming area and none of the other guards would have even blown their whistle at him. And most of them probably thought that the motions he was making—waving and shouting—were just playing. Certainly the counselors and campers thought he was playing—or just trying to get attention.

He wasn't playing. I knew it with every part of my body. I stood up on my chair, blew three quick blasts on my whistle, and hit the ground running.

When a guard gives that signal, the other guards know to react quickly to clear the area and wait for instructions. They don't question the guard who calls the signal; they look to see how they can help. Every kid was out of the water and rounded up in under three minutes. But by that time, I was far out into the lake, running until the sand gave way, then kicking for all I was worth. I felt the slight undertow just where the sandbank leveled off. It wasn't strong enough to drag me, but it was strong enough to drag a little kid like Andy. He went under just as I reached him.

It seemed like the longest ten seconds of my life until I reached him. I quickly brought him to the surface, and shoved my rescue board under his arms to keep his head up. I know exactly how long it took me because the other guards were there in a boat as I surfaced and one of them had to call the time. They pulled us into the boat. Andy's eyes were wide open. I thought they were following me, but I must have imagined it. He wasn't breathing; his lips were blue. I knew what to do and I did it.

By the time we got to the shore, the paramedics were there but Andy was breathing just fine. He was, however, crying hard. He put his arms around me and wouldn't let me go.

"Sam, Sam," he kept saying over and over. "I'm so sorry! Am I gonna get in trouble? Will they let me come back?"

Poor kid! He was afraid that everyone would be mad at him! I was so sad and so angry then. His counselors should get in trouble for not making the other kids play with Andy, for not making someone be his buddy. If anyone had been nice to this kid just once, he wouldn't have left the group. I wrapped my arms around him and held him close as we pulled onto the shore.

Later, my supervisor told me I had done an outstanding job. Then he said, "Sam, I was watching the beach from the tower. I saw that kid. He just looked like he was playing and waving. How did you know so quickly that he was in trouble? By the time I realized it, he was already under but you were in the water."

How had I known? To someone who has been doing it all his life, waving for attention doesn't look anything at all like drowning. Drowning is what kids with ADD feel like they're doing when they're not even close to the water.

The other guards made a big deal about the rescue and for once in my life, I was the hero, instead of the loser.

Everyone said it was a miracle that I had saved Andy. It was a miracle that I had been there in the first place, a substitute guard with ADD, kicked out of my other program and forced to take a life-guarding class. I had been put there because I could see when a kid like Andy was drowning, not waving.

From a distance, they look the same. You have to get close to see the difference. ✳

*My parents got divorced when I was* nine. It took me a while to get used to the quiet after my dad moved out because it was such a contrast to the yelling and screaming my parents did when they were together.

We went to my dad's house every weekend and he always did fun stuff with us—movies and ice cream, amusement parks, bowling. I always looked forward to seeing him.

My sister Molly is four years younger than I and she loved going to my dad's house, too. The truth is my dad is a great guy. My mom is great also, don't get me wrong. But there is something special about the father-daughter relationship.

Everything changed when my dad began dating Lisa.

I was almost fifteen when he introduced us and it shocked me to learn that he had been going out with her for almost a year. It never entered my head that he would *ever* want to go out with a woman other than my mom.

So it was a complete shock when, only three weeks after he introduced us to Lisa, he announced that they were engaged. Worse, Lisa had a daughter exactly the same age as Molly, and Lisa wanted Molly and Sarah to be junior brides-maids in the wedding!

I hated Lisa! Everything about her annoyed me. It was as if

she was trying to establish her ownership of my father. And the worst part was, my dad let her!

We never went anywhere just the three of us—Molly, my dad, and me. Lisa and Sarah were always included. I began to feel like the fifth wheel, and I found myself thinking up reasons not to go places with them. I pretended to be sick. If they were going to a restaurant or to the movies, I'd stay home and watch TV and make myself a peanut butter sandwich. And think of ways to break them up.

Lisa asked me to go with her to look at wedding dresses. I couldn't believe she had the nerve! But my dad took me aside and asked me as a special favor to him to go with Lisa. I couldn't say no.

We went downtown to the bridal department of one of the nicest department stores in the city. All the dresses were so fancy—lots of pearls and lace and "tulle"—that's the name of this material they use for brides' dresses. It looks like mosquito netting.

Lisa kept asking my opinion. I wanted to scream at her, "I don't care what you wear! You're ruining my life! You're taking my dad away from me."

Instead I sat in the corner and kept quiet, giving only the barest of replies to anything I was asked. Couldn't she see that I didn't want anything to do with this wedding? That I didn't want her in my life? We had been doing fine without her. Now everything was going to change!

After about the millionth dress, Lisa found one. Of all the dresses she tried on, this was the most beautiful, and even though I would never admit it, it was perfect on her. It didn't even need any alterations. The store boxed it for Lisa and we took it home.

We went out to lunch, just the two of us. And Lisa started to talk to me. "Tina, I know you don't like me very much, but I would like us to try to be friends if for no other reason than to please your dad. You know I love him very much and I will try to make him happy!

"I'd like us to try to be a family. You know I was married before. My first husband died when Sarah was just a baby. She's never had anyone but me. This is hard for her, too." If that was supposed to make me feel like being nicer to them both, it didn't.

She changed the subject. "Let's go look for a dress for you, now!"

I wanted black. I thought it would be most appropriate for the way I was feeling. I settled for navy blue.

When we got home, I took my dress up to my room and threw myself on the bed. I had been due for a good cry for a long time and this was the time.

I must have slept for a while because when I finally opened my eyes, it was dark out and the house was quiet. My head hurt and my eyes burned. I walked into the kitchen. There on the table was a note. "Tina, we went out to dinner and to the movies. Will be home by twelve. There's pizza in the fridge. Love, Lisa."

*Love, Lisa!* That did it! I didn't love her, I hated her! Who was she trying to fool with such a note? She didn't love me!

She just wanted my father!

Well, I'd show her! But how? Then I knew! Her wedding dress! Without even thinking clearly, without even knowing exactly what I was going to do, I picked up the kitchen scissors and went upstairs.

The dress was hanging up on the back of the bedroom door. I wanted to slice the whole thing to ribbons! I wanted to ruin her wedding day just like she was ruining my life!

I started with the side seams and I cut carefully every thread up and down both sides. Then I stepped back to admire my handiwork. You couldn't even tell. There was just enough thread to hold the whole thing together. The day of the wedding, when she went to put that dress on, it would fall apart in her hands.

I put the scissors back where I got it and ate the pizza. Then I sat down to watch a movie and wait for them to get back.

But somehow I couldn't settle down.

They came home around eleven-thirty and Sarah and Molly went up to bed. Lisa said, "Thank you for going with me today. I know how you feel—and I know it was a tremendous effort on your part to go with me, and I want you to know how much I appreciate it. I want to ask you something—would you be my maid of honor? Please?"

Maid of honor? Shame washed over me. I didn't know what to say. Somehow I didn't feel so mean toward her anymore. I guess I had taken out all my rage on her dress. What had I done?

As the weeks went by and the wedding approached, I began to take a good hard look at my dad. Lisa was right. She did make him happy. I guess I had been so wrapped up in myself that I hadn't noticed that he needed love and companionship from anyone other than his kids. When he was with Lisa, he seemed more relaxed and he laughed more. I told Lisa I would be her maid of honor.

About a week before the wedding, my dad and I went out to dinner, just the two of us.

He told me how much he loved me, how nothing and no one would ever change that. He said a lot of other nice, sweet dad-things but I didn't hear them. All I could think about was how mean I was, how hateful. I was planning to ruin what would be not just Lisa's day but my dad's day, too. What a monster I was!

It was only a few days before the wedding. How could I undo the damage? I can't sew. I can only destroy!

Please God! I prayed that night. There must be a way out of this! If you won't do it for me—I know I don't deserve a miracle—then please do it for my dad and Lisa. They don't deserve to have their day ruined just because of me!

It happened while we were all in the kitchen. Molly and Sarah decided to try on their dresses, and they begged Lisa to try hers on, too.

I held my breath. Should I tell Lisa? Should I let her try it on and then pretend to be as shocked as anyone when the dress came apart at the seams?

To my utter shock, she came down that stairway looking like, well, exactly what she was supposed to look like—a radiant bride. The dress never looked better! Maybe . . . but as Lisa turned, I saw one single hanging thread. The dress was only just holding together.

I was about to open my mouth to tell her everything when it happened. Sarah opened the refrigerator door, intending to take out the water pitcher. Her hand brushed up against the ketchup bottle—that was the only explanation any of us could come up with afterward. That bottle sailed out of the fridge and plopped open on the floor. It was plastic so it didn't break. But the ketchup splattered over the floor and onto the one dress in that room that reached all the way to the floor—Lisa's beautiful white wedding gown!

She was too shocked to cry or scream. Nobody moved.

This was my miracle! "Lisa, take it off quick! I know there's a great cleaners near where my mom lives. I'll take it over there and they'll know just what to do!"

She was still in shock so she didn't even question me; she did just as I said, stripping down to her underwear there in the kitchen. I grabbed the dress and was out the door in a flash.

I ran all the way to the cleaners. When I got there, I was so out of breath that I couldn't speak. But I didn't need to. The lady who owns the cleaners doesn't speak much English, but she understood immediately when she saw the ketchup. She said only, "When is wedding?" I gasped, "Two days!"

"You come back tomorrow. Don't worry. I fix fine!" She turned around and disappeared into the back of the store before I could tell her anything about the seams.

They were just about to close and the lady's son hustled me out the door, saying, "Don't worry. My mother will fix the dress. My mother is miracle worker."

He had no idea how much I hoped he was right!

The next day, Lisa went with me to pick up the dress. The lady brought it out with a big smile on her face. "See, I told you! I get stain completely out! Good as new!" We paid for the cleaning but with Lisa standing there, I had no chance to ask the lady if she'd noticed the ripped seams, if she'd *really* made that dress as good as new.

What better place to say a prayer than in a church? As the wedding began, I asked God to please let the dress be all right, to please make the whole day be beautiful. For all of us.

Everyone cried. It was perfect. They were away for a week, and Sarah and Molly and I stayed with my mother. We really got to know each other.

When they came back, I watched them unpack. I watched Lisa put her stuff in the dresser next to my dad's stuff. And I didn't feel bad at all.

Lisa took out her wedding dress. "I am going to take this to the cleaners and have it 'antiqued.' That way, it'll be preserved in case one of you"—she pointed at me, Molly, and Sarah— "wants to wear it."

Just as she said it, she noticed the thread. "Oh, look what must have happened at the reception . . ." Before I could say a word, she pulled the thread!

Well, it was a *perfect* wedding! ✳

*he camp I have been going to since I was* nine years old is nestled deep in the Wisconsin pines. It's a beautiful place far away from the city, noise, parents, school, and other things that most kids don't want to think about during the summer.

I have a ton of memories from camp. I have albums and albums of camp pictures and each one reminds me of something wonderful that happened.

After my senior year in high school, I returned to camp as a counselor. It was the summer I had waited for all my life. Being a staff member is the most fun.

I chose to be a counselor up on the hill for the kids going into ninth grade that year. Even though I was only three years older, they looked to me to be their role model. At one point during that summer, they even looked to me to save their lives.

Tornadoes are common in northern Wisconsin during the summer months. In fact, it's a regular camp activity to go with the local fire department "trackers," specialists in predicting the paths and severity of tornadoes when they chase a tornado. It's spectacular! From a distance, we can see the whole thing from the flat farmland floor to the top of the whirling funnel.

Camp has never been directly in the path of a tornado but we have gotten torrential rains and winds when one has hit the area. We have shelters built especially for those times when we are warned to take cover. We have always felt very safe in our shelters and just thought it was very exciting.

The summer that I was a counselor, we tracked two tornadoes with the local fire department. We learned the difference between a tornado "watch" and a "warning." A "watch" is when weather conditions are right for a tornado to occur—when air pressure and temperature collide. A "warning" is more ominous—it means a tornado has been sighted in the vicinity and that those in the area have to be prepared to take cover.

We learned what to do in case of a tornado and we often had drills so that the kids would find the whole thing exciting and not frightening.

The summer that I was the counselor we learned one more thing about tornadoes: They are completely unpredictable.

I personally learned something else—to trust my own instincts!

It was particularly hot and humid. The temperatures had been in the nineties for over a week and the campers had to be wet all the time. When we weren't swimming, we had water balloon fights or just hosed each other off. Every game and sport was played with everybody drenched. But nobody minded. That was part of the fun of camp.

When we got the news from the local sheriff's office that there was a tornado "watch" on, we weren't particularly surprised. Rain had been predicted and we were actually looking forward to relief from the intense heat and humidity that had hung on us for days.

I sent my group to the showers to clean up before dinner and checked with my supervisor who was manning the telephone and radio. "No change in the tornado status," John told me. He wasn't the slightest bit worried.

They say that animals have a sixth sense about danger. Humans are animals, too; we just don't always listen to our own sixth sense because we don't have to. But the minute I walked out of our tent into the open air, I felt it.

The hair on the back of my neck stood on end. So did the hair on my arms. I looked at the faces of my campers and my fellow counselors to see if they felt it, too. I couldn't believe that not one of them showed the slightest bit of concern.

Clearly, as if the voice were quite close to me, I heard, "Run, don't walk, to the underground shelter!"

I felt fear then. As I entered the dining hall, I ran up to the counselor who was making announcements and just screamed, "Everybody into the shelters, now!" And to my complete amazement, everyone did just as I said. I think the kids probably thought it was a drill like so many others we had had. The other counselors just thought I had been told to call a drill. Only my supervisor knew that he hadn't told me to act this way. He ran over to me and started to say something.

I thought something in my face must have stopped him because he opened his mouth and then shut it with a pop.

Later I would find out that it wasn't my face that stopped him. It was the huge black funnel shape he saw out the dining room window directly behind me.

It came from out of nowhere! We only saw the first rain and lightening as we all scrambled down the steps into the shelter under the dining hall. The last counselor down pulled the heavy door shut and we were plunged into darkness. Then, the counselors switched on the emergency flashlights and called roll to make sure each camper was accounted for. With each "Here" called out, I prayed that no one was up there left behind.

Everyone had done his job and all the kids and counselors were accounted for, which was a good thing, because in another second, we heard what could only be compared to 100 supersonic airplanes overhead. It was the loudest noise I'd ever heard! And it seemed to last forever. The air in the shelter became close—almost as if fear had created an electrical charge, like static electricity. I still had the image in my mind of the hair on my arms standing on end.

To keep the children from panicking, we began to sing songs. We sang and sang. After we were all hoarse and tired, I noticed that the noise overhead had died down. I looked at my watch. What seemed an eternity had, in fact, been twenty minutes.

The radio crackled to life, ". . . one of the worst twisters to hit northern Wisconsin. It has moved off to the east now and will soon lose itself over the Great Lakes. Where it came from, we don't know. Residents of Waushara County are safe now . . ."

My supervisor went up first. He didn't come down to get us right away and then when he did, his face was ashen. The lights in the shelter had come on, and I watched John's face as he struggled for words.

"We're all okay, campers. Don't worry. The storm is moving on but it was a real tornado. What you will see above might scare you, but please remember that we are all safe."

Nothing John or anyone could have said prepared any of us for what we saw as we came upstairs. As far as the eye could see, there was not one building standing anywhere on that campground, anywhere on the hill.

Every cabin, every tent, bed, cabinet—all gone. Trees had been uprooted and lay across every path and trail leading to and from the dining hall. Even the office building, which had been made of stone, was gone, reduced to a pile of rubble.

But every one of the 150 campers and staff on the hill at Camp Mohanchi was alive and well.

Even though every one of the campers called home to tell his or her parents that he or she was safe, no one insisted on going home. Instead, carloads of parents and friends began arriving the next day with camping equipment, clothes, food, and bottled water. They set up tents in a clear area and proceeded to help with the cleanup and rebuilding of the camp. The county and the neighboring towns sent crews to repair power lines, water pumps, and sewage systems. In less than a day after the work started, Camp Mohanchi was back in business!

A scientist who studies weather told me when I received my award from the sheriff of Waushara County that there is a scientific name for the phenomenon I experienced. It has to do with a change in barometric pressure. I heard his words only as "Blah . . . blah . . . blah." I knew that the name for what happened was "miracle," pure and simple.

One of the items recovered when all the rubble was cleared was a collection of photo albums that the camp office had kept through the years. The albums were completely dry and undamaged. They, like all of us, had been spared.

I guess that's what they mean when they say, "Camp memories are meant to last forever." ✳

*My little sister always annoyed me.* She would get into my stuff, tell my friends and boyfriends things I wished she wouldn't, and play dress up in my clothes, shoes, and makeup.

It took me a few years before I realized that she just wanted to be me.

Kate is six years younger than I am and when she was a baby, she almost died from whooping cough. I remember the sound she made at night when she first got sick, before my parents rushed her to the hospital. It's an awful "whoop-whoop." It sounds like someone trying to breathe and scream at the same time and not being able to do either.

For a long time, I worried that she would die, and I had nightmares. But as I got older, things gradually returned to normal. I forgot that she had been so sick and I treated her just the way any other big sister would treat a sibling six years younger. First she was my plaything; then she became a nuisance. My parents said that one day, we would be friends.

Kate is a really good listener and a good friend. When she was about four, she had a friend named Melissa who didn't speak clearly at all. Most four-year-olds have a little baby lisp but Melissa was really hard to understand and it frustrated her. Once when she was playing with Katie in our family room, I heard Melissa tell Kate about a trip her family was taking to "Bizzywowo." Katie sat there for a minute, not saying a word. I knew she didn't understand her friend and neither did I. Then Kate said, "Oh, Melissa! I wish I could go to Disney World with you! Will you get me some Mickey Mouse ears?" Katie had thought about what Melissa said until she finally understood her. Even at four years old, Kate was like that, always attuned to other people.

It was like that with the older couple who lived next door to us. The Kelleys have lived there since we moved in when Kate was born. I just thought of Mr. and Mrs. Kelley as the nice older couple next door. Kate, however, made friends with them. She went over to visit with them and made them little presents and brownies. My mother once asked Mrs. Kelley if she minded, but Mrs. Kelley just showed my mother her refrigerator. On it were several of Katie's handmade pictures along with some of her school pictures. The Kelleys enjoyed having a little girl around long after their own kids had grown and gone. I suppose she was like their granddaughter.

Mr. Kelley had a stroke in the spring of my senior year of high school. He wasn't that old—maybe in his sixties—and he had always been a very smart, well-read man. He also had traveled a lot in his job and knew a lot about different subjects. Katie thought Mr. Kelley was very interesting. He always taught her something she wouldn't have learned in school.

After Mr. Kelley had his stroke, he had trouble speaking and it made him very frustrated.

But Kate had an amazing amount of patience. The same powers of understanding that she had used with her four-year-old friend, Kate now used with Mr. Kelley.

One night in the middle of the summer, Kate came into my room. I was up late reading, but I put my book down when I saw my sister's face. I knew she wanted to talk—really talk.

But Katie didn't just sit on my bed and start in. She walked all around my room, picking up stuff, looking at it but not really seeing it and putting it down. "Kate!" I finally said, "You're making me nervous! Settle down! What is wrong with you?"

"Anne, I wish I knew," she said tearfully. "I just feel like something is wrong. I can't put my finger on it."

"I don't feel well," she said. "Anne, can I sleep in here with you tonight? I'll just put my pillow and blanket on the floor." I said okay and helped her bring her stuff in. We both fell asleep quickly.

She woke me up. And not gently! "Anne! Get up! Now!" I thought she was having a nightmare but her eyes were wide open. The clock said two-fifteen.

"Next door!" said Kate, "We have to go next door!" Then she called out for my mom and dad. I thought they would be angry with both of us for waking them.

My dad appeared in our doorway in his pajama bottoms. Before he could ask what was wrong, Kate pushed past him, grabbing his arm and pulling him. "We've got to help them!" she said.

We got all the way to the kitchen and we smelled it before we saw it. Thick black smoke was billowing out the back kitchen window of our neighbor's house! My mom reached for the phone but my dad was out the door before I knew what was happening. I did the only thing I could think of—I put my arms around my shaking sister.

My dad is not a big man but I saw him use his whole body to break down the Kelleys' back door. He disappeared into the Kelleys' house just as I heard the sirens. By the time the fire-fighters had unloaded and rushed into the house, my dad had already reappeared at the back door with Mr. Kelley in his arms.

The paramedics took Mr. Kelley from my dad's arms and laid him on a stretcher. Then I saw them bring Mrs. Kelley out and do the same for her. Within minutes, the fire was out. It was only in the kitchen and it was all over within a few minutes. They were the longest few minutes of my life.

We watched as both the Kelleys received oxygen. We breathed a sigh of relief as we saw that Mr. and Mrs. Kelley were both giving the paramedics a hard time, trying to pull their oxygen masks off. At least we knew they were alive!

Katie scrambled out of my arms and ran over to Mr. Kelley as he was being loaded into the ambulance. She said something to him. He seemed to relax and nod at her. After that, he didn't fight the paramedic anymore. Katie ran back to us standing in the doorway of our house.

"What did you tell him?" my mother asked.

"I told him that he could breathe easy, now."

Now I suppose that to the casual observer that might seem like a pretty standard thing to tell a man whose house had just been on fire. But Katie had chosen exactly those words for a reason.

She told my parents and me as we sat around the kitchen table, unable to go back to sleep. "It was a terrible feeling I had. It started before I went to sleep in Anne's room. I couldn't put my finger on it but it was a feeling I'd had sometime before, maybe a long time ago. I couldn't breathe and I couldn't talk. Even after Anne let me sleep in her room, I tried to forget about it but I couldn't. Each time I laid down, there it was again!"

*I couldn't breathe and I couldn't talk.* Was that what Mr. Kelley was feeling as he lay in bed?

And then Kate said something so amazing that for a moment, it seemed the temperature in the kitchen had dropped twenty degrees.

"Daddy, I felt that way before. When I was a baby, I couldn't breathe and I couldn't tell you what was wrong because I couldn't speak! Don't you remember?"

Of course we remembered! It was when Kate had whooping cough. But how could Kate remember? She had been only a couple of months old.

Dad tried to explain it to us all the next day. He said there was a perfectly good scientific explanation for how my twelve-year-old sister had remembered a feeling she had experienced as an infant. He said that there was also probably a perfectly understandable reason why that sensation had come back to her at exactly the moment when our neighbor was experiencing exactly the same thing—*the inability to breathe and to speak.*

Dad went on for quite a while explaining. I don't know why he bothered. It was really just so clear. It was a miracle, pure and simple. Even we kids could see that.

She still wants to borrow my clothes and get into all my stuff. I'll let her do that while I'm away at college. I'll even let her sleep in my room while I'm gone. Most sisters keep in touch by phone calls and e mail. But with my sister's special gifts, I don't know if we'll even need those ways to communicate! ✳

$\mathcal{W}$hen my older brother Josh was diagnosed with a rare form of leukemia, my whole family was devastated. Josh has always been the one who makes everyone laugh, who always has something nice to say, and who can find someone's best points even when they may not be obvious to the rest of the world. He's also amazingly good-looking and I'm not just saying that because I'm his sister. All my friends think so, too. With his thick black curls, deep dimples, and piercing blue eyes, Josh could get a job as a model easily.

When he first was diagnosed, everyone was surprised, especially Josh, because he didn't feel that bad. He had gone to the doctor for his regular checkup so that he could play sports in school. A weird bruise on his leg tipped the doctor off and after some tests, we were told that Josh had acute mylogenic leukemia. Chemotherapy would begin immediately. Instead of starting his senior year of high school with his classmates and friends, Josh was admitted to Children's Hospital at the beginning of September.

Josh kept all our spirits up. Even while horrible drugs dripped into veins in his arms, he cracked jokes and made us think about other things. His friends weren't allowed to visit him while he was having treatment, but they sent huge stuffed animals and lots of letters. We held each of his gifts up to the window of his room while he was isolated so he could see them. And, gowned and gloved, my parents took turns reading letters and cards from all his well-wishers to him.

For a while, it seemed that Josh would get better. We all kept waiting for the test results that would tell us that Josh's leukemia was in remission. I grew to hate that phrase—"test results."

Finally, we got the news we had been hoping for—Josh's blood levels were in the normal range. Though thirty pounds lighter and bald, my wonderful big brother was able to come home and resume his life again. The first thing he did was to tell a joke he had heard while he was in the hospital. He may have lost his hair but he hadn't lost his sense of humor!

It took Josh a long time to regain his old strength, so he only went to school part-time. The rest of the time he spent on one of his favorite pastimes—the computer. Like everyone else in my family, I didn't think anything of it until one evening, Josh called me over.

"Rebecca, I want you to see this. Now, I don't want you to be upset, but we have to be realistic. I've been doing a lot of research on the Internet about my type of leukemia. Everything I've read says that the cure rate for guys my age and from our family background . . . well, it's not as good as it is for other groups of people."

"What are you saying?" I cried. "Don't you feel well? The doctor said—"

He cut me off. "Shh . . , calm down! I know what the doctor said, and yes, I feel okay now, but I had to see what all the research shows. I just have to know. I'm as sure as you are that I'll be cured. With everyone praying for me—how could it be otherwise?" He smiled but his eyes were sad.

Josh's remission didn't last long. By January, he was back in the hospital and the doctors were trying another set of drugs on him. I watched him through the window of his room. Only my parents were allowed in with him. My mom's eyes above her mask were wet with tears as she put her gloved hand over Josh's. When he could no longer manage even a half-hearted smile at her, I turned away.

It was the most awful thing in the world to see my big brother, the mainstay of our family, waste away. And it hurt to see my parents' anguish. I wanted to do something to help them, to help Josh. I prayed as hard as I knew how.

The doctors told us that Josh's only hope was a blood transplant. It was a dangerous procedure, used only as a last resort. It involved literally draining all the blood from Josh's body and then refilling him with a bone marrow donation. "Sounds a little like filling the car up, doesn't it?" joked my big brother.

Everyone in our family volunteered to donate bone marrow and we are a big family. The doctor told me that I would have the greatest chance of success because Josh and I have the same parents. I really wanted to be Josh's bone marrow donor. But the test showed my blood wouldn't match.

I almost got hysterical when I heard that. How could it not match?

Josh was put on a waiting list and his name went into a computer where all his information and data were compared to those of donors worldwide.

A week after we began our search for a donor for Josh, we got a call from the hospital. I saw my father go into his study to take the call. When he came out, he had tears in his eyes but a smile on his face. "There is a match for Joshua! It will come from someone in Israel!"

Israel! So far away! I wondered who would be a match for my brother in Israel when I, his own sister right here in the United States, wasn't.

"Let's just be grateful that there is someone to help us, Rebecca," my father said. "We prayed to God to make a miracle for Josh. I guess we couldn't specify where that miracle came from." My father smiled at me.

I didn't care where it came from either. But it still made me wonder.

Josh received his transplant on a Friday. He would stay in the hospital for up to a month to rule out any signs that his body was rejecting the transplant.

After seeing Josh one afternoon, my father came home with a funny expression on his face. He gave me a piece of paper with some writing on it. It was a Web address.

My father is not computer illiterate, but here he was, asking me to look something up on the Internet for him. He paced back and forth behind me while I logged on and went to the site.

I understood the minute the page came up. There looking back at me was a picture of—if not Josh, then certainly Josh's twin! The young man whose picture appeared at the top of the page had the same dark curls, the same gorgeous dimples, and the same beautiful blue eyes as my brother.

His name was Adir and he was twenty-one. He had created his own Web page to tell about his life in the Israeli Army. I scrolled down, barely reading any of the details. Then it finally dawned on me why I was reading about a kid in Israel who just happened to look like my brother. He must be Josh's bone marrow donor. I looked at my father sitting in his leather chair. His face was in his hands.

"Dad, is this who gave Josh the bone marrow? They look so much alike! Do we know him?"

My dad took a long time to reply. My mother came into the family room and sat on the sofa, waiting for my father to speak.

"I think," he began, "that that boy is your cousin. When the doctors got the match through their registries, it was so exact that they thought we might be related. I sent Adir—he pointed to the screen—"an e-mail asking him about his grand-parents."

I sat back in my chair and let out a long sigh. My father's parents were Holocaust survivors but as far as we knew, neither of them had had any brothers or sisters.

*As far as we knew.*

Adir's father e-mailed my father back later that night. There is an eight-hour time difference between Chicago and Israel, but my dad wouldn't go to bed until he heard that little voice say, "You've got mail!"

I wish I could describe the joy on my father's face when Adir's father told him that he was the grandson of my father's brother. There had been six of them born in that generation—all boys. We had always thought that my grandfather had been the only surviving member of his family—and his brother thought he was. Now, we learned that my father had a first cousin who lived in Israel and had eight children! Adir was the oldest, like Josh.

I could write a book about what my grandparents said when they found out. I could write a book about how joyful our reunion with everyone was when we visited Israel after Josh had recovered. I could write a book about how blessed my family is. We asked for one miracle—my brother Josh. But we got more—an entire family!

Of course, my father thinks it's also a miracle that his father learned how to use the Internet—to talk to his brother in Israel! ✳

*We've always been a close family.*
Actually, every family I know who is from Mexico is close—and big! It's a good thing, too, because we watch out for each other. The neighborhood where we live on the far Upper West Side of New York City is known to be rough. There are a lot of gangs and kids just looking for trouble. But, there are equal numbers of us who look out for one another's mother or sister or kid brother. It's just the way we do things in Spanish Harlem.

My uncle, Tio Angelo, has lived with us ever since I can remember. *Tio* is the Spanish word for "uncle," but to me, it's just part of his name. He's only a few years older than I am, but I've always called him Tio Angelo.

Tio Angelo doesn't speak English very well despite the fact that he's been here almost eighteen years. He says it's because he doesn't have to; all his close friends speak Spanish. I think that's the reason he can't get a really good job. Tio Angelo is really smart. But smart in a street kind of way. He just knows things—things you don't learn in school, like how long you have to work loading trucks to get enough money to pay the rent but not so long that you get bored or worse, the boss begins to ask questions about your green card.

Tio Angelo had a friend who had a good job. He told Tio

Angelo that he would get him an interview. I know that his friend had arranged things so Tio Angelo could work there without worrying about immigration. Tio Angelo was really excited the day he had to go for the interview. He had to be there at nine o'clock in the morning. Normally, Tio Angelo hates getting up that early, but I knew he would be on time. He works hard for our family. He loves us—especially my mother, his sister—very much. I had to get to school early so I didn't get to say good-bye and good luck to him before I left.

Tio Angelo's interview was at a restaurant in the World Trade Center on September 11, 2001. Through no fault of his own, Tio Angelo was a few minutes late.

I was already at school when I heard that two planes had crashed into the World Trade Center. But what happened next can only be described as mass hysteria. Even though my school is way up north and not close to the World Trade Center, they told us to go home. It wouldn't have mattered if we had permission or not. I knew my mother would need me.

The streets were packed with people. Everyone was crying, holding each other. When I reached the building where I live, my mother and all of our neighbors were outside. My little brother held on to my mother's skirt and sucked his thumb. He's three and a half and we've been trying to get him to stop. But I didn't say anything to him about it when I saw the look on his face.

My mother screamed when she saw me and threw her arms around me. I tried to tell her not to worry, everything would be all right. I was pretty stupid, I guess. It's just that, until I got home, I didn't know that the Twin Towers had fallen and that no one had heard from Tio Angelo.

That day was the longest day of my life. But we were all together—not just my family, my mother and my brother and sisters, but the whole building. We all kept our doors open and people kept coming in and out. Every mother and grand-mother started cooking. I don't know why exactly, but it seems that's what they do in times of crisis—they cook. And, somehow all that food gets eaten.

The TVs were on in every apartment and with the doors open, the noise was unbelievable. My mother kept looking at the clock. She was waiting to hear from her brother.

My family is very religious. At least, my mother is. She prayed hard that day and even though I'm not so religious, I prayed, too. We asked for a miracle.

Many hours later, our miracle came home—Tio Angelo was covered with a gray dust so thick that the only thing you could make out on his face were the whites of his eyes. He was terrifying to look at—the wild expression on his face, the blood on his hands and clothes. My mother thought he was the most beautiful thing she had ever seen.

My mother screamed all sorts of questions at Tio Angelo, not giving him time to answer. What happened? Where was he when the planes hit? Why did it take him so long to come home? Was his friend safe?

Tio Angelo took a long shower. When he came out, he

looked more like himself. Then, he told us what he did for the fifteen hours since the terrorist attack. He was saving lives.

Tio Angelo had been outside when the towers were hit. He heard the planes overhead and looked up to see the first one slam into the north tower. Within minutes there were firemen and police cars and trucks all over. He saw the buildings come down.

Tio Angelo started to run, like everyone else. But he saw a lady stuck in some debris. He pulled her out and carried her to an ambulance. He said he didn't know if she was alive or not. But, after that, he said, he knew he couldn't leave and come home. He stayed to help.

Tio Angelo told us all this very matter-of-factly. There was a strange calmness in him. He didn't seem terrified, but I couldn't imagine how he could not have been.

He told us some firemen yelled at him to get away. One of them yelled at him in Spanish. Tio Angelo told the fireman, "I can help. I'm strong." Tio Angelo didn't leave.

My uncle saved several people that day—an elderly man, a woman, and a businessman in a suit. Tio Angelo remembers him especially because the two of them were about the same age. He put his arm around Tio Angelo's neck and called him, "My brother." Tio Angelo ran with all of them as far north as Houston Street. Then he stopped to catch his breath.

A lot of people in New York speak Spanish. But Tio Angelo said that that day, it didn't matter. Down there at the south end of Manhattan, everyone was speaking the same language. Tio Angelo didn't tell us that it was the language of fear and terror.

He said it was the language of people helping each other, calling each other, "My brother."

Tio Angelo never talked much about it after that day. But I could see that the whole thing changed him. He's been quieter. He speaks more slowly. But some things about him remain the same. He still watches out for his family, just like he did when his family included every single person he saw on the street that day. He works hard—at paying jobs when he can get them, at home helping my mother and our neighbors when he can't.

"Tio Angelo" means "Uncle Angel." Someone or something saved my Tio Angelo that day, saved him from being just a nameless, faceless statistic, an undocumented person who died in the terrorist attack on New York City. And instead of being that statistic, Tio Angelo became an angel, one who walks here on earth. I know there's a reason he was saved. Maybe he's still got something important to do here on earth for us, for our family. Or maybe he's destined for bigger things.

I'm not religious but I believe in miracles. And I know that somewhere in this big, impersonal city of millions, there are at least three other people—including a young businessman who called my Tio Angelo, "My brother"—who believe in them, too. ✳

*I* was about five and my little brother was two when my parents found out he had autism. He did dumb things like banging his head and stacking the same blocks in exactly the same order over and over again. He cried a lot, too.

I learned that his needs came first. If I was watching TV, Jimmy might watch, too, but he would stand right up close to the TV and I would have to find another place in the room to see the set. My parents rarely moved him. They said he didn't understand.

But Jimmy understood a lot more than my parents thought he did. One time, he came into my room when I was doing math homework, memorizing the multiplication tables. There was no other way to do it than to keep saying it aloud: "five times six equals thirty, five times seven equals thirty-five," and so forth.

Jimmy sat on the floor. He has this habit of repeating what other people say. It's called echolalia. You can't tell whether Jimmy really understands something he hears or if he is just repeating the word because he likes the sound. When I let him try some of the problems I was working on, he solved them in less than half the time it took me. And he did it by repeating the multiplication tables out loud.

Jimmy could play the piano. If he heard a song on the radio or even if he heard someone humming it, Jimmy could play it with both hands on the piano. The only thing he did when he played that was strange was that he counted aloud while he played. He had his own peculiar rhythm and he heard his own special music.

But there were so many times when it was impossible to reach Jimmy. He had lots of therapies—speech, physical, and occupational—that taught him to use the skills he did have. But a lot of the time, he would sit by himself and play with some object that he loved. He wouldn't look at you. Jimmy's teachers tried to explain to me what it was like to have autism. They said that Jimmy's mind is locked up tight in his own little world. He stays there because he feels safe there. He can't relate normally to the outside world. I tried to imagine what my brother must feel like but it was hard.

When I was a junior in high school, I was part of a youth group that did a lot of outdoor things. We went camping, rock climbing, and horseback riding. We spent some time working on a local farm picking corn and taking care of the animals. We repaired and built things, too, like fences and barns. It was a great program because it got you outdoors and it taught you useful skills. That was why my parents thought it would be good for Jimmy when he was old enough.

They never even asked my opinion.

Being part of that group was a big part of my identity. My friends were in it. I was popular and respected for my skills and my smarts. I loved my brother but he wasn't like other kids; he required a lot of attention and I didn't want to be the one to give it to him. I just wanted to be Mark Dalton, normal teenager, not Mark Dalton, brother of Jimmy, the autistic kid.

Mr. Geller, our group leader, encouraged my parents to bring Jimmy into the youth group with his own counselor. Mr. Geller felt that with the counselor, Jimmy would be fine. It might have worked except that when we went anywhere or did anything, Jimmy didn't want to listen to the counselor. He wanted to be with me.

"Marky sit with Jim on the bus. Marky ride horse next to Jim. Marky . . . Marky." Jimmy insisted on my being with him all the time. And he would become very agitated if I wasn't.

My girlfriend, Lisa, was more tolerant than I was. She liked Jim and didn't mind his hanging around with us. She brought him treats like candy and gum. But she didn't treat him like a baby. He was fourteen and she sometimes talked to him as if he were a normal fourteen-year-old, asking him about sports and girls. He always smiled at her and sometimes when he answered her, his answers made sense.

Jim did one thing that really annoyed me when our group went on trips. If I took another seat on the bus, even one row in front of him, Jimmy would say over and over, "Marky, here I am! Marky, here I am!" It was as though Jimmy thought I just hadn't been able to find him. It was hard to make him understand that I wanted to sit with Lisa and he should sit with his counselor and his own age group.

One weekend in the spring, the youth group had planned a camping trip to Wild River.

The campsite is surrounded by beautiful woods and there are several rock formations that the older kids are allowed to climb. The camping trip is one of the highlights of the year. And even though several grown-ups come along as chaperones, the kids do everything—we build the site, set up the tents, build the fire, and cook the food.

Despite the presence of the grown-ups along, Lisa and I managed to sneak off by ourselves to watch the sunset from the top of a rocky crag.

I don't even remember what started the fight between Lisa and me. One moment we were making out on top of the hill; the next minute she was angry. She left me on the hill and went back to camp. I was mad, too, and I wanted to teach her a lesson so I didn't start back right away.

I looked out across the valley. It was really breathtaking. And the air smelled like pine. I must have been more tired than I realized from the climb up the crag because I fell asleep.

I awoke with a start. It was very dark! They would certainly be worried about me. I was going to be in big trouble. I sat up and, like the good camper I was trained to be, sat very still and tried to adjust my eyes to what little light there was. I knew better than to start moving in just any direction. I had to keep my wits about me, stay where I was, and wait for help.

I tried not to panic, but being alone in the big woods at night is pretty scary, even for a seventeen-year-old.

Taking a deep breath, I calmed myself and strained to see in the dark. I couldn't even see my shoes. Think! I told myself. Think clearly and logically and you'll get yourself out of this, I thought to myself. But all I could think was Stupid! Stupid! To let myself get in this situation! How many times had I heard Mr. Geller lecture us? You don't wander off! You don't leave the group! Stay together! But, no, I had to be alone with my girlfriend! What was wrong with me? Why hadn't I been thinking?

The temperature drops rapidly in the dark, and I shivered despite my Tec Vest. I struggled to stay calm. It was just so dark! If I could only see which direction I was facing, I would know which direction camp was. But there was no way of knowing and I had been sitting at the top of a mountainside. I couldn't risk getting farther from camp or, worse, falling down the slope.

Where was the moon? Its light didn't penetrate the thick branches of the pines. I felt swallowed up in the darkness, small and alone.

Strangely, I began to feel safe, as if the dark were wrapping me up. There could be any number of dangers in the dark, but I didn't feel their presence. What was it I did feel?

My body curled tight, I began to rock back and forth. I felt . . . I felt like Jimmy! Or at least how I imagined Jimmy must feel. It was the first time I had ever thought how it must be to be autistic, to have some sense that there is a world around you, yet you are unable to enter it and so you detach yourself from it. I stayed in that position a long time, rocking back and forth. . . . It felt comfortable to rock. It felt safe and familiar in a place where nothing outside of my body and mind did.

Jimmy! He must be terrified, not having me around at the campsite. I hoped they thought up a real good excuse why I wasn't there.

It began to get colder. If the temperature continued to drop, I might be in real trouble. I could feel my panic rising.

Curled tight into a ball, I tried to erase all the negative scary thoughts about the world around me. I retreated into myself, just as I supposed my autistic brother did.

And then I heard him. My brother Jimmy had obviously joined the search party for me because I heard him loud and clear, "Marky! Marky! Here I am!" I turned in the direction of his voice and took two steps. How typical of him to tell me where he was rather than call for me to tell him where I was.

"Marky! Marky! Here I am!" I walked about ten feet toward his voice. That's when I saw the glow of light from the rangers' and Mr. Geller's flashlights. I heard Mr. Geller shout into his walkie-talkie: "We found him! He's all right!"

"I'm sorry," I said before Mr. Geller could start yelling at me. To my surprise, Mr. Geller just grabbed me and hugged me.

"You're in a lot of trouble, son. But your folks are going to be very relieved that you're okay." I looked around for Jimmy. "Where is he?" I asked.

"Who?" Mr. Geller asked.

"Jimmy, of course! I heard him calling me."

Mr. Geller eyed me strangely for a long minute. "Mark," he

said. "You've been out here a few hours and it's cold. Your mind is playing tricks on you. That's a dangerous sign. Good thing we found you when we did. When I left, Jimmy was asleep in his tent with the other kids. You must be hungry. That's what your problem is, I bet!" Mr. Geller put his arm around me and led me back to camp. The other kids, including Lisa, made a big deal about me. I had only been a mile or two away the whole time.

But a mile or two is too far to hear the voice of your brother—your autistic, loving, sensitive, living-in-a-world-of-his-own brother who was fast asleep, as I saw with my own eyes when I got back to camp. I gazed down at Jimmy. He slept with his arm up over his eyes as if he was shutting out the world. Just as I had done in order to be able to hear his voice telling me where he was so that I could get back to him.

And I was there, right next to Jimmy when he opened his eyes in the morning. ✳

*I was already partway home from* school when I remembered that my mother had asked me to pick up a cake mix and some eggs to make a cake for my little sister's birthday. I have to take two different city buses to and from school, which often takes me almost an hour each way. I go to a special school in the city for kids with vision problems. I have retinitis pigmentosa and, though I can see, my vision is limited and my night vision is terrible.

So I was nervous to get off the first bus in a strange neighborhood and go to a grocery store. But I had to do it because my sister would have been very disappointed and my mother would have been mad at me. When we passed an A & P market, I got off at the corner. It wasn't too late. I hoped it wouldn't take me too long to run my errand and then get back to the bus stop. With any luck, the next bus would come along quickly and I would get home before dark.

I was standing in the checkout line behind a well-dressed lady who was fumbling around in her purse for something. Then she paid and walked toward the door. I moved forward to the counter, and as I did, I stepped on something. I looked down to find a beautiful gold-and-diamond wristwatch under my shoe. It must have fallen off the lady in front of me! I saw that she was just opening the door to leave and I ran after her. "Hey, lady! You dropped this!" She turned around, and when she saw what I was holding, she quickly touched her wrist. "Oh, my God! I knew that catch was broken! Thank you so much! You don't know how much this means to me! May I give you a little something as a reward?"

I told her no. It was a beautiful watch and I was sure that lady could have given me a nice reward, but it didn't feel right to take anything. I told her I was just glad I found it and to have a nice day. She asked me my name. I told her and she shook my hand and thanked me again.

I had a great story to tell my mother and sister as we ate our cake after dinner. And that was the end of it. Or so I thought.

Two years later, I was graduating high school. My eyesight had not worsened but I was still limited. It was always my dream to become a teacher, and I wanted to go to Teachers College in the city. Maybe I would be able to help kids like me, with low vision. But my mom worked hard to support my sister and me and there wasn't any money for college. I didn't even have to ask.

I was an okay student, not the best, but not the dumbest. But I knew I wasn't going to get any scholarships. There were plenty of kids at my school who also had vision problems and who got much better grades than I did even though I was a hard worker.

So I was not just surprised, I was shocked when my advisor

called me into her office one day toward the end of the school year to tell me that I was going to college. It wasn't a scholarship from the school. Someone had personally arranged to pay all my expenses so that I could attend Teachers College!

"Cara, I'd like you to meet your benefactor," my advisor said. She introduced me to a nice-looking young man, who looked vaguely familiar to me. My advisor explained that he owned some property in the city, and as she spoke, I realized that I had seen this man's picture in the newspapers. He gave away lots of money to charities every year.

Then he said, "Two years ago, in a grocery store you returned a watch that my mother had dropped. I had given that watch to her on her birthday and she loved it. When she gave it to me to get the catch fixed on it, she told me how this nice young lady named Cara had returned it to her after it fell off in a grocery store. She described you as having vision problems and we asked around to see if you attended a special school. We have been keeping track of you for these last two years, and now we would like to pay you back for your kindness and honesty."

I couldn't believe it! Because I had forgotten groceries that day and had to get off the bus in a strange neighborhood, I had been able to return that lady's wristwatch. And now, I was going to college as a result of just doing a simple good deed.

I guess it's true—one good turn deserves another, but sometimes God gets involved to put you in the place where you can do that good turn. All that and He made sure I got home before dark and my sister had a birthday cake! ✳

*In our state, you get a driver's license at* sixteen after having had a learner's permit and a driver's education course.

When I turned fifteen, I got a part-time job after school and on weekends. I wanted my own car so badly I would have taken any kind of job to earn the money. My parents had made it clear that they would not buy me one or pay for my insurance.

I didn't care. Whatever job I could get, I took. I turned sixteen in June.

My dad helped me find my car—a great one! I put a great sound system in it and drove it to work all summer with the windows down and the music blaring. What freedom! I was careful to watch my speed anywhere I thought there might be a cop, which was everywhere in town.

But there was a big stretch of open highway about five miles outside of town, where the city ended and the countryside began. All the houses out that way were farms, and they were acres apart. At night, it was pitch-black because there weren't any streetlights or traffic lights—no side streets intersected the highway. It just seemed to run from the edge of town straight out to nowhere. It was the perfect road to travel on if you needed to be alone, away from everyone and everything. The perfect road to escape on.

As it turned out that summer, I needed to escape. John— a kid I went to school with, a kid with everything going for him, a kid just like me—got drunk at a party and drove his car into a cement guardrail. The cops couldn't find any skid marks at the scene to suggest that he even tried to brake.

After the funeral, everything was different. It wasn't that John had been my best friend or anything. He wasn't. But it was just that he seemed so normal, not depressed at all. It scared the hell out of me.

Had he deliberately killed himself or was it an accident? No one could say for sure, and the mood of the town changed a lot that summer. The volume of the music the kids played was softer. People spoke more quietly and seemed more serious. My parents kept telling my brothers and me how much they loved us. And they constantly warned me about drinking and driving.

I never told my parents that I had been at the same party as John that night, doing the same thing John had been doing, the same thing all of us kids had been doing. I couldn't tell them. I couldn't talk about it even with the other kids who had been there.

After the accident, we left the liquor alone when we got together. Driving became my favorite form of entertainment. I discovered that patch of highway, and I often went out to drive there after I finished work and before I went home. I'd drive as far as I could until it was time to turn around and get home.

Driving was my escape. It made me feel almost high. I tried not to speed, tried not to be stupid, but I felt like nothing could hurt me when I drove that car. Out on that highway, I could escape the memories of that awful night. I could escape the fear I felt each time I passed the place where John had died. I drove that country highway so often, I knew every pothole for ten miles.

I didn't like driving around town, past the familiar places— places where John and I had done our normal things. There were so many reminders. I couldn't get it out of my head that John and I had so much in common. Our lives were virtually the same—we had nice families and the same friends. We liked the same activities, played the same sports. *I couldn't get it out of my head that I had been drinking at the same party that night! It could have been me.*

I suppose if I had talked about it, I would have been better off. If school had been in session, they would have had grief counselors to help us; everybody would have had to go and it wouldn't have seemed like a big deal to talk to someone. But I didn't want anyone to know what I was feeling. I couldn't even be sure what it was I was feeling—scared, confused . . . responsible maybe?

The week before school started, the pools closed and there was a party on my last day of work. After all the lifeguards and staff cleaned up the pool, put away all the lounge chairs and cleaning equipment, we broke out the food. Someone had ordered pizzas and soft drinks. Someone else had brought chips and other junk. And someone brought beer.

I didn't touch it, not one sip. But it made me nervous. Suddenly, it was as if I was back at that other party again. The party that had been like all the others except for the fact that a kid just like me had taken a drink at the party, then left that party to plow his car into a guardrail.

I had to leave. I got into my car and headed out where I knew I could shake this awful feeling, this awful sense that I should have done something, anything to stop a kid from killing himself.

I didn't care that it was late and my parents might worry. I didn't care that it was so dark, I couldn't see my hand in front of my face. I had driven that road a thousand times all summer during broad daylight. I knew every inch of it. Nothing would happen to me. Nothing except maybe I would lose this terrible pent-up helplessness.

My headlights lit the road and I sailed over the smooth pavement. It felt great.

That's when I saw the flashing lights. At first I couldn't tell where they were coming from. There was something in my rearview mirror but the light also appeared to be in front of me. I slowed; then stopped.

I realized I had been speeding. Trying to outrun all the demons that were in my head, I had done what I had promised myself I would never do—speed! I looked out at the cop as he approached my car.

It was so dark that I couldn't see his face. What I could see in the light from the flashlight that he pointed at my car was his silver nameplate. *John.*

In all the times that I had driven this road, I had never seen one cop. It unnerved me to see that his name was John. But John is a very common name.

But I was shocked when he said, "I don't know what it is you are trying to get away from, son. But you were on your way to a body bag just now. Don't you know the highway is under repair just up ahead around that curve? The road ends in a ten-foot drop. At the rate you were going, you wouldn't even have felt the pavement end before you found yourself in space. Shame to mess up such a nice car, too."

What was he talking about? I had driven this highway all summer. There weren't any road repairs. There wasn't even any curve in the road. He made me get out of the car. I thought he was going to either cuff me or give me a breath test. Instead, he pointed his flashlight up ahead and made me walk with him.

Ten feet from where my car stopped was a wooden saw-horse—red and white, with a yellow reflector—the kind you see when roads are under construction. Just beyond the sawhorse, not five feet farther, was the end of the road.

*The end of the road.* I sat down where I was and in the dark, John put his hand on my shoulder. "Sit here as long as you need to, son. Then go home and talk to your folks." Then he climbed into his squad car, turned it around, and drove off.

I don't know how long I sat there alone in the dark at the

edge of a highway under construction. I guess I sat there long enough to realize that I had just been saved, been given a second chance, that some Being had decided it wasn't my time to die. It was my time to live.

But you can't really live until you put all your demons to rest. I had a lot of demons inside me. I went home and told my dad what happened. I had to wake him up to talk, but he didn't mind a bit.

The next day, my dad and I drove out on the highway. I wanted to show him the spot where the cop had stopped me. I told my dad everything. I talked so much that we didn't realize how far we had driven until we got to the state line.

In the daylight, there was no curve in the road, no repairs being done, no ten-foot drop where the highway ceased to exist. Had I imagined it all? Was "John" a real cop or an angel sent to make me stop, to make me begin to heal, to put all my demons to rest?

The only answer was that when my dad and I drove it together, every inch of that highway was intact. And so was I. ✳

$\mathcal{S}$omerset County, Pennsylvania, is a rural area, mostly farming and mining towns. But we have had more than our share of miracles. And some of my friends and I feel that we helped bring one of them.

On Wednesday, July 24, 2002, nine coal miners became trapped in the Quecreek Mine, about ten miles from my house. Rescue efforts began immediately and everyone in our small town either was or knew someone involved in the rescue effort. My friends and I, like most other people in the nation, did the only thing we could think of to help—we prayed.

Fifteen of us from our local church and high school staged a prayer vigil. Many of us are sons and daughters of coal miners ourselves.

But nothing seemed to work. At first, rescue workers knew the men were alive because they had special equipment that detected tapping noises. But those noises stopped at around 11:00 A.M. on Thursday morning. Huge drills were brought in to get to the men. The plan was to make two shafts—one to serve as an air shaft and another, larger one to use to pull the men out. The drills had to burrow through 250 feet of solid rock. But one of the drills, which weighed about 1,500 pounds, broke off 100 feet down into the shaft and got stuck. It would take hours to free it and start drilling with a new bit flown in by special helicopter.

Time was running out. We all knew that those nine men were down there submerged in water at least up to their waists. Water pumps had been brought in and were pumping water out of the mine at a rate of about 20,000 gallons per minute! And it would be extremely cold. In addition, the lights from their helmets would last only about twelve hours from the time they became trapped. By Thursday morning, they would be in complete darkness! Add to that the fact that the men had no food and no drinkable water . . . it was terrifying.

Some of the girls in our prayer group began to cry when the governor of our state said that the situation looked grim. Everyone could remember at least one or two other mining disasters in our area where people died. It's a hard profession, a hard life.

We tried to think of other ways to help. Many of us had gone to offer help to the workers, bringing food and water and blankets. But it wasn't enough. We knew we needed a miracle to save those men.

That's when the idea hit us—three or four of us at the same time! Maybe God needed to hear the message about those nine men from someone other than us. Maybe we needed some angels to speak for us!

Somerset County was the scene of the crash of Flight 93 on September 11, 2001. The remains of those passengers and crew members had long since been sent to their final resting place, but the spot where the plane went down is marked to memorialize them.

At 9:00 P.M., my church youth group drove out to the crash site, about ten miles in the other direction from the Quecreek Mine. There, we linked hands and prayed to the angels on that plane—the brave men and women who had sacrificed themselves to prevent Flight 93 from becoming a missile like the other three planes that had killed almost 3,000 people in New York and Washington, D.C., on September 11.

We brought only flashlights and water. Nothing else—no radio or battery-operated TV to keep us in touch with what was happening just a few miles away at the mine. We wanted it to be just us and God out there in that field. About an hour after we started praying, the wind picked up for just a moment. I glanced at the lighted dial on my watch—10:16 P.M. Then I bowed my head again and continued.

We prayed hard, every one of us. Then, in the wee hours of the morning, something happened. I couldn't put my finger on what I felt, exactly—it was like a shiver running up my spine. As I looked around our circle, I knew the others had felt something, too. Even those of us who were dozing off snapped to attention! Again, I looked at my watch—2:45 A.M.

It wasn't until the sun rose that we found out: Turning on the radio in one of the trucks, we learned that at exactly 10:16 P.M. the night before, the rescue workers at the mine had broken through and been able to drop a telephone down into the shaft. They learned that all nine of the miners were alive and well!

*10:16 P.M.!* The moment I felt that wind and glanced at my watch!

But the next part of the newscast really caught my attention: At 2:45 A.M., the last miner was pulled from the shaft. I knew it wasn't a coincidence. I had felt it and so had *every* one of the others in our prayer group at *exactly 2:45 A.M.!*

All nine men were present and accounted for. The people around the mine's entrance must have been whooping and crying for joy! But miles away, by the side of the road near an entirely different miracle site in Somerset County, four trucks were parked, caravan style. Nineteen local high school students stood in the middle of the road and also whooped and cried for joy!

No doubt the prayers of the entire nation helped God decide to make a miracle here in western Pennsylvania. And maybe He thought that since we had already witnessed one tragedy, He would spare us another. But things had looked so bad during the rescue . . . until our group decided to pray to the angels of Flight 93. Maybe God needed to hear from them to get the message to reach down and scoop out nine honest, good coal miners who were just doing their job.

President Bush praised the coal miners and called the way they behaved toward each other while they were trapped, "The spirit of America."

I call it Americans helping Americans.

*hen God saves a life, He usually leaves* the details to others. In my case, there were so many individuals and so many extraordinary events that came together to save my life that no one, not even the worst skeptic, could doubt that God himself orchestrated the whole thing.

On January 22, 2002, I was shot by a terrorist on a street in Jerusalem. That was the day I died.

I loved being in Israel. I had worked hard to get there. During my senior year in high school, I worked every day after school and then every day during the summer to pay for a year of study in Israel after I graduated from high school.

Even though the situation there had worsened, I returned to Israel for a second year. I was never afraid. Israel was going to be my home. It was already my homeland.

That day in January started out normally. I went to classes and afterward, with my friend Shoshana, I went to the El Al ticket office in Jerusalem. I had planned to visit a friend of mine who lives in London and I went to purchase my ticket. Shoshana and I went to a bus stop on Jaffa Road to wait for the bus that would take us back to school. I was excited that I had my ticket in my hand, and I called my friend in London to tell her that I was coming.

Much of what happened next was told to me weeks after the attack. Mercifully, I don't remember anything about it. But the details were related to me by my friend Shoshana and by many other eyewitnesses who survived this terrorist attack that killed two people and injured forty-six.

He shot me point-blank in the chest. The bullet entered my left lung and exited my back.

He was eventually shot and killed, but while he was still spraying bullets in every direction, an ambulance from Magen David Adom arrived to pick me up. Three minutes had elapsed since I had been shot.

Three minutes. An eternity. But what came next was a series of miracles that proved beyond any doubt that there is indeed power in prayer and goodness in the hearts of strangers.

Paramedics Dror Schisshiem and Dr. Ricki Kaplan performed emergency lifesaving procedures. But Dror realized quickly that I was losing blood too quickly to be able to make it to the primary trauma center at Haddassah Hospital in Ein Kerem. He told the ambulance driver, Shai Shapiro, to take us to Shaare Zedek Medical Center, ten minutes closer. Ten precious minutes.

Shai tried to radio ahead to Shaare Zedek to alert the emergency staff there to expect us. But his radio wouldn't work! Thinking fast, Shai used his cell phone to call his wife, Annie, a nurse in the open-heart operating room at Shaare Zedek. She answered on the first ring.

"Don't talk, just listen," Shai commanded. "Stop whatever

you are doing and prepare for this patient!" He described my injuries. What he didn't tell her was that, at that moment, I had no pulse.

Because of Shai's phone call, I was taken immediately to the operating room on arrival.

I had been shot at about 4:10 P.M. When I arrived at Shaare Zedek at 4:25 P.M., I had bled out.

Dr. Maher Deeb was the doctor who made the decision to try to save my life. A senior cardiothoracic surgeon, Dr. Deeb had the most experience with injuries like mine. In his experience, only about one or two in 100 could survive. He made the decision to give me the chance to be one of the lucky ones.

They broke three of my ribs to get to my heart and lungs. Clamping the pulmonary artery in my chest, they were able to restart my heart and pump me full of blood again.

But the bullet had lodged in my lung. So the doctors removed my lung and wired my ribs back together again. I had been without oxygen for several minutes. Brain damage was a possibility. In addition, the doctors were also concerned about the risk of infection since the surgery had taken place so quickly, without time for all the normal sterilizing procedures.

Dr. Deeb, who made the decision to bring me back to life, is an Israeli Arab. As I recovered, Dr. Salah Odatallah took over my care. He even accompanied me back to the United States when I was able to travel. He wanted to ensure that I would not have a bad reaction to flying given the fact that I had only one lung. Dr. Salah is also an Israeli Arab.

I often wonder what would have happened if Dror Schissheim hadn't decided to go to Shaare Zedek instead of Haddassah Hospital? What if Shai Shapiro hadn't had a wife who happened to be an OR nurse at Shaare Zedek and who, for some unknown reason, had left her cell phone turned on so that she was able to receive her husband's call? What if I had arrived a minute later? And what if Dr. Deeb had looked at me and seen only a girl with no pulse or vital signs and decided to give up on me?

He told me later that he looked at my face when I came in. He saw on that gurney, a nineteen-year-old girl who still had a lot of life in her. A nineteen-year-old girl who wanted to live, to study and learn, to grow up and have a family someday. A nineteen-year-old who deserved a chance to live.

I walked out of that hospital on February 3. My physical recovery would take a long time. I have a scar on my chest and one on my back. And I suppose I have some scars that aren't visible to the eye.

But one thing I know for certain. In this world, where there are some who hate and want to hurt others, there are an equal number who want to help others and to save lives. And God rewards people like that by allowing them to play a part in working a miracle now and then. People I will never even meet offered prayers for my recovery. Everyone involved in my ordeal told me that their faith had been renewed by the experience of having saved a life. They got a powerful message, as did I: Those who kill may destroy human beings but they can't touch the human spirit. Only God can do that. ✳

*I*ve always lived on a farm and though I like to go see a rock concert in Chicago or visit some of the museums or amusement parks in the big cities, I prefer the life our family has on the farm to anything that the city has to offer.

My sisters and I take care of the animals. That's a job I love. I'll probably be a veterinarian when I grow up. I think I understand animals better than I do people.

It's especially true about Maggie, a horse my father gave me after she was born to our broodmare, Queen Elizabeth. Watching a birth like hers makes you know there is a God. The way such a big thing, a perfectly formed little horse, first grew inside and then just kind of slid out of her mother, well, it is a miracle.

Maggie was dainty and delicate and looked like she could be a good hurdler. I think my parents expected me to train her for that kind of riding. But I wanted to train Maggie dressage. Dressage is a special type of training that requires an unbelievable bond between horse and rider. The horse actually has to sense the rider's desires because she isn't given much in the way of hand control or signal. Dressage originated in the French Army. Soldiers had to have their arms free to aim and shoot rifles, so their horses had to know to respond to subtle shifts of a rider's weight or leg pressure. Watching dressage performed is like watching figure skating. Points are awarded in competition based on balance, obedience, and suppleness.

Every day before school, I fed and brushed Maggie. Then I would let her out to pasture. Horses like Maggie graze most of the day. Only workhorses like Maggie's brother, Charlie, get fed protein and oats and barley. Charlie needs the extra calories.

After school, I trained Maggie. She was so graceful and so responsive. We were really tuned in to each other!

I had other farm chores after school, such as fence mending. Every farm kid I know knows how to mend a fence by the age of twelve. It's an important job because if there is a hole any-where along the back acres, an animal will find it and get lost.

One hot humid June day just before the end of my junior year in high school, my dad sent me out to fix the fence at the top of our property. I finished exercising and brushing down Maggie and put her in the bottom pasture. Then I saddled up Charlie and took my equipment and went to look for the fence posts my dad said needed repairs.

The air was heavy; a storm was coming but I thought that I would have enough time to fix those holes before the rains came.

You can tell how far off the storm is by how long after the lightning you hear the roll of thunder. I saw the sky light up in the distance and figured the storm to be a good three miles off. There was plenty of time for me to fix the fence. I found the hole pretty easily right where my father said it was, at the top of the rise overlooking the low pasture where Maggie and the other horses were grazing.

Every farm kid knows several things about storms. They can come up suddenly, and if there is lightning, you want to be as low to the ground as possible and not near any tree or metal object. But what most people don't know is that lightning can strike well before the rains come.

It struck the metal fence post before I felt it in my teeth. If I had been touching the fence, I would have been a goner. As it was, I only got a secondary shock. It was enough. I heard the clap of thunder at the same instant. It sounded as if a grenade had exploded and it spooked Charlie so badly that he took off at a gallop down the hill. Horses are smart. Charlie knew to seek low ground.

I tried to stand and found that I couldn't move the entire left side of my body!

That's when total panic swept over me. I had only felt a momentary pain so I hadn't thought I was badly hurt, just stunned. I figured I would walk back to the stables. But I couldn't get my body to work. Would my dad know to come look for me? I felt very exposed lying there at the top of the hill. I could still be a strike target. It is absolutely *not* true what they say about lightning not striking twice in the same place. Oh, I prayed that my dad would know to come get me quickly!

I thought about Maggie. I wasn't worried about her in the storm. I knew she would head in to shelter. Lady that she was, she hated being out in the rain.

Years of training had put Maggie and me on the same wavelength. But, I reminded myself, that type of communication only occurs between horse and rider, when they are in *physical* contact. Maggie was safe in the stables and I was there, high up on the hill! There was no way she could know I needed help, was there?

Just as I felt a searing pain, my dad and our neighbor were there with the flatbed truck.

They told me later that they knew to come looking for me even before they saw Charlie come back riderless. They knew, my dad said, because Maggie refused to go into the stable. When the rains started, she had come into the paddock but she stood pawing the ground and shaking her head up and down. Normally she's the sweetest, gentlest of animals. But no amount of coaxing or pulling could make her come inside.

"That darn horse—she looks pretty and ladylike," my dad said later at the hospital. "But let me tell you she's powerful stubborn when she wants to be. She wouldn't move one step forward until we saw Charlie. Now, I gotta tell you that if I had just seen ol' Charlie come back without you, I might not have moved so fast because you know, sometimes we just slap that old boy on the rump and he comes right in by himself. But the way Maggie was carrying on—well, I knew you were in trouble. And you know what? The minute I let go of Maggie's bridle and took hold of Charlie's to bring him in, Maggie quieted right down and walked in all by herself! It was almost as if she knew that she had given me the message to go get you and then she could relax. How do you like that?"

I liked it fine. ✳

*N*oah and I grew up together. We've been best friends for as long as I can remember. Oh, we went through that thing where I thought all boys had cooties and he hated all girls just because they were girls. But we were always together. When my dad built me a tree house in our yard, Noah was the only boy I allowed in it even though he wasn't content to play inside it like I did with my girlfriends. He had to jump down from it, screaming out, "Geronimo!" and scaring everyone half to death. But that stopped when he broke his arm and my mother told him he couldn't jump anymore.

Noah and I ended up at the same college. That wasn't really so unusual because a lot of my graduating class went to the state university. But it's a huge school. Since I am an English major and Noah is premed, we realized that if we wanted to keep up with each other, we would have to make a date to actually sit and talk.

We got together at the student union about once a week. Both of us, like most of the student body, studied in the library until ten o'clock. Then most kids took a break. The student lounge would be jam-packed at that time. If you really wanted to talk, you had to leave the building. Noah and I usually arranged to meet at the entrance to the library. We often just walked around for an hour before going back in to finish studying or, more likely, just gather up our books and go relax for a while before it got too late.

College life suited both of us. We were working hard and liking it. And for the most part, we both steered clear of the alcohol and drug use that was a typical campus scene. At least I did.

Toward the middle of our second semester, I noticed a change in Noah. He didn't want to get together as often, and when we did, he wouldn't talk much. I asked him what was wrong but his answer was always the same, "Nothing."

It wasn't nothing. I began to hear from mutual friends that Noah was having a terrible time with his studies. He had always talked about going into medicine, and he was really good in the science classes we took in high school. But college was so much more competitive. A really close friend of Noah's called me one day to tell me that Noah had failed his Organic Chemistry midterm. I knew he needed someone to talk to. I knew he needed me. But he didn't call, and when I called him, he brushed me off.

A few weeks went by and I didn't see or hear from Noah. Then we ran into each other in the bookstore. I was shocked at his appearance! He had lost a lot of weight and it showed most in his face. Noah—sweet, handsome, fun-loving Noah—looked about 100 years old. He had taken up smoking cigarettes. He lit up the minute we walked outside together.

"What's happening to you?" I begged him to tell me. "You

were always so health conscious. You were the one to tell me that cigarettes and that other stuff are for losers. You were going to be a doctor! What are you doing to yourself?"

He got angry. "What do you know about anything? You think this is easy? Well maybe I'm not going to be a doctor after all. Maybe I don't have what it takes. And so what? Who cares?"

I never got the chance to tell him, "I care." He threw his butt into the street and walked away.

Days went by, then weeks. I saw Noah only a few times around campus and he ignored me for the most part. I thought about calling his parents but I was afraid that I would worry them needlessly. After all, what could I tell them? That Noah looked terrible? That he started smoking? That I was worried to death about him? No parent wants to hear that. And anyway, I knew that Noah's parents were having troubles of their own. My parents told me that Noah's parents were thinking of divorce.

As we approached finals week, I saw Noah a few times around campus. He actually stopped me and talked for a while. I noticed that he wasn't smoking—at least he didn't while he was with me. One bright sunny afternoon, I saw him at the cafeteria and invited him to go for a walk. I knew he didn't have a class until three so I thought we'd have a chance to catch up.

I asked him how things were going, if he felt better. "Yeah, as a matter of fact, things are better. My parents probably are getting a divorce, but I guess I've come to terms with it. There isn't anything I can do about that. Don't worry about me, Barb. I'll be all right."

His words sounded good and he looked much better than he had in weeks. I tried to feel reassured. He even kissed me on the cheek when he said good-bye. He was dealing with life, I thought, wasn't he? *Wasn't he?*

It came to me while I was leaving the gym after swimming. It was only a brief thing—a flash really. But I saw it clearly: an image of Noah jumping out of my tree house and yelling, "Geronimo!" And it made my skin crawl.

As I walked back to my dorm, I tried to tell myself that I was being ridiculous. Noah seemed much better than he had in months. Why should I have an image of him as a child, and why should it make me feel so uncomfortable? I told myself that the goose bumps on my arms were probably from the cool air on my skin after just having exercised.

But that didn't explain the sinking feeling in the pit of my stomach. As I opened my door, I saw it again! Noah, as he had been at five years old, jumping down and screaming, "Geronimo!" He had been happy then—even as he jumped at least fifteen feet and broke his arm.

I ran as fast as I could. Noah's dorm was way across campus. His room was on the third floor. My heart was pounding in my chest as I dashed up the three flights and raised my hand to pound on his door.

To my surprise, the door swung open. There on his bed sat my best friend, his head in his hands, crying pitifully. I walked over and sat down next to him, wrapping my arms around him. I didn't say a word. There was no need to. The wind blew in gently from the open window.

"How did you know to come?" Noah finally asked me after he had calmed down, after I had closed the window, after I had called the mental health advisor on campus.

Should I tell him about the "vision" I'd had of him when he was five? I just told him, "That's what best friends are for." ✳

After my little sister was born, my parents bought a big old house in the suburbs and we prepared to leave our beloved apartment in the city. I say "beloved" because it was the only home I had ever known.

But I admit I did like the idea of having my own room, and when I saw the big old Victorian on the wide shady street that my parents had chosen, I decided that suburban living had its advantages. When our parents took my brother and me to see the house for the first time, they had to make special arrangements with the lady who still lived there. Her name was Mrs. Tilden and she was a character.

When she first opened the door, I was really surprised. I guess I expected a hunched-over old lady from what my parents had told me about her. After all, the house we were buying was over 100 years old and had been in her family for generations. It needed a lot of work—everything from new plumbing to painting and carpeting. I assumed that the reason the house was in such bad shape was that the lady who owned it was too frail and old to take care of it properly. Boy, was I wrong.

Mrs. Tilden spent so much time traveling and playing golf, tennis, and volleyball, that she just didn't have time to keep up the huge old Victorian.

She threw the door open wide when we rang the bell and I thought she was going to throw her arms around us as we walked in. "Hello! Hello!" she sang out. "Welcome to your new home—almost. Well, dear," she said, turning to me, "I suppose you'd like to see the house and choose your bedroom? Come, come right this way!"

Mrs. Tilden took us into the kitchen and poured some lemonade. We sat down and she told us that she was glad such a nice family was going to live here. She said that she had had several offers on the house before ours but had chosen us because she just had a "feeling" that we were the right ones to live here. She said that she had even discussed the sale of the house to us with her mother, a lady in her nineties who lived in a private nursing home. She said that despite her mother's age, she still had "all her marbles" and Mrs. Tilden always consulted her on every major decision.

Mrs. Tilden's mother had grown up in the house, been married in it, and moved back to raise her children when her own parents moved to Florida after they retired. As Mrs. Tilden talked about her family, I imagined them right there in front of me in turn-of-the-century dress, very elegant and formal. I have a very vivid imagination but I couldn't help it. The house and the family who lived there seemed very exciting to me.

As we were about to leave, Mrs. Tilden handed my mother a camera. "Do take some pictures, my dear," she said. "You'll want to have some before and after shots." My mother took a lot of pictures of the kitchen and the bathrooms, since those were the rooms where the most work was going to be done. As we were leaving, I shot two pictures of the living room just to use up the roll. My parents expected to leave that room pretty much the way it was. I was glad. It was perfect just the way it was, with a big stone fireplace and tall ceilings with lovely old moldings.

When we left to go back to our apartment, I was happy thinking about the move. By the end of the summer, all the work would be complete and we would be settled.

The next day, my mother came into my room where I was lying on my bed looking at magazines for ideas to decorate my new room. My mother handed me the roll of pictures that she had just had developed. "Here, Beth," she said. "You keep these and then you can take the pictures after we finish redecorating."

I looked through the "before" pictures. Something about the two of the living room caught my attention. Maybe I was just letting my imagination run wild again, but I could swear that against the back wall was what appeared to be a shadowy outline of a person! It was impossible to tell if it was a man or a woman, but the figure appeared to be kneeling on one knee.

When I told my mother, she just said, "Oh, it's probably just a light reflection or something. Maybe there was a mirror in the living room and the flash from the camera just bounced off it." But I had been in that living room. There was no mirror there.

Maybe there was a ghost in our new house. I wasn't frightened by the idea. Actually, I thought it was pretty neat. But as I said, I do have a vivid imagination.

My mother told me that Mrs. Tilden would be all moved out by the end of the week and the reconstruction would start the following week.

I didn't think anything more about the pictures or the move until we went to the new house to inspect the work being done several weeks later.

As we stepped into the front hall, I half expected to feel a creepy sensation as if my "ghost" was there waiting for us. But of course I didn't. All I felt was excitement and pleasure at how beautifully our new house was shaping up. I loved it.

The workers had refinished all the hardwood floors on the first floor and the house smelled of varnish and newness. We walked into the kitchen where the construction crew was busy installing new cabinets. The crew foreman saw my mom and held out his hand. "Look, I found this in the old plumbing of the kitchen sink. I don't imagine it's worth anything, but I thought your daughter"—he pointed to me—"would like to have it."

It was an old ring, a thin band—very tarnished and very bent—but with one tiny pearl in it. He dropped it into my hand.

When we got home, I put the ring on my dresser and started to get ready for bed. I don't know why but something made me go into the hall and get the "before" photos of our new house. I looked again at the ones that seemed to have my "ghost." Whatever it was now didn't seem very scary or supernatural to me. Oh well, I thought. I probably just made up the "ghost" before because I was looking at the photos right after leaving the old house and hearing Mrs. Tilden's family stories. I figured I was seeing what I wanted to see.

But the next morning, my mother said, "Beth, don't you think we should give Mrs. Tilden the old ring? I'm sure it belonged to someone in her family." We made plans to go out to see her later in the day.

Mrs. Tilden had moved into a beautiful condominium where she could play golf and tennis and swim to her heart's content. It wasn't very far away from her old house. She was a little breathless when she answered the door.

"Sorry! I was just on the phone with my mother. I'm going to visit her today. Did you say you had something for me? What is it? Some mail? I thought I gave the post office my forwarding address."

I held my hand out and showed her the ring. She didn't recognize the ring but she did take it, telling us she would ask her mother about it later in the day.

A month after we moved in, Mrs. Tilden called. She said she would like to come over, that she had something to tell us. She asked my mother specifically if I was going to be home.

We sat in the kitchen and had cookies.

Mrs. Tilden told us quietly that her mother had passed away the week before. "Ninety-two and never sick a day in her life! She died in her sleep, not a bad way to go," she said. She was certainly not overcome with grief. But she did seem sad and I had the impression that she would miss her mother very much.

Then she said, "The ring you found was buried with her. It was her wedding ring and she lost it in this house when she was a new bride. It wasn't worth very much. My dad bought her a new one years later that was solid gold and had diamonds all around it. I have it now. But my mother told me how much she had missed that ring with the one tiny little pearl. It was all he could afford when they were young, and she was heartsick when she dropped it down the kitchen drain. She told me that over the years, they had taken that drain apart, modernized the plumbing, and even replaced the sink a few times, but they had never found it. She could hardly believe it when I took it to her after you returned it to me." Mrs. Tilden's eyes grew bright but she did not cry.

"You know, it was almost as if she was waiting for that ring to come back to her before she could die. And then, once she had it, she could relax and let go. She's never stopped missing my father even though it's been almost twenty years since he died. I guess now she can be with him." Her face took on its old happy look. "Maybe she didn't want to face him until she had that ring back and now she can! What do you think?"

I thought it was a great story and I told her I was glad we had been able to find the ring and return it to her.

I told her what I thought I had seen in the living room photos. Somehow I didn't feel foolish telling her even if it was really just my imagination hard at work. Amazingly, she didn't laugh at me or anything! Instead, she nodded her head as if it were the most natural thing in the world. "That must have been my father walking around this house looking for that ring. You say he was kneeling in the living room? Well, my mother told me often the story of how he proposed to her—on one knee just like in the movies!" She looked over toward the back window. "Over there. That's what my mother told me—he proposed right over there, and he gave her this little tin ring that probably cost next to nothing but which meant everything to both of them."

I could see them clearly in my mind's eye, two young lovers about to begin their life on earth together. It had taken a miracle and the "right" family to find that ring, but I knew without a doubt that those two lovers were now beginning their lives together in another world. ✳

*O*ur high school requires a certain number of community service hours prior to graduation. After 9/11, my graduating class of eighty-five students wanted to do something that would be especially meaningful. We live in a small town in western Pennsylvania, not far from where Flight 93 went down and most of us, along with our families, couldn't shake a deep sense that the world had changed forever and not for the better. We all became much more aware of the news and all the lead stories were terrible and tragic—war in Afghanistan and the Middle East, crimes and scandals. What could we, as high school seniors, do that might help us—and maybe some others—heal?

Our class came up with the idea of a "Hope Balloon Send-Off." Everyone in the class would write a personal message of hope. It did not have to be directed at anyone in particular. It could be a prayer to God, a poem, or a story—anything from the heart of the sender. The messages would be signed, "The student body of Archwood High School." Each message would be placed into a red, white, or blue balloon. Then we would launch the balloons, sending them into the sky, not knowing where they would land but imagining that our messages would somehow be heard.

When we told our school principal about our idea, he thought it would work perfectly as part of our school's scheduled Wellness Day. That was a day when professionals in many different fields came to the school to talk to students about ways to keep themselves mentally and physically healthy.

After four years of high school, I had seen friends who did drugs, stopped eating, and engaged in any number of activities that threatened them physically and mentally. We were all concerned with the normal pressures of life—getting into college or getting jobs, dealing with relationships and personal self-esteem. After 9/11, it seemed more and more of us were feeling especially depressed. The Hope Balloon Send-Off was a chance to write your feelings—and this is why I think it was an immediate hit—everyone wanted to feel hopeful again.

Wellness Day was in January when the sky was gray and the weather was cold and miserable. It was a perfect day. Not only did the whole school turn out, so did most of the town. The mayor spoke and so did our principal. Some clergy did, too. Everyone had something positive to say. As we stood there on our high school football field, we all felt united and proud.

The school band played and we all sang patriotic songs. At just the right moment, the balloons were released. It was a spectacular sight! Sure, we realized that our balloons would likely pop somewhere just out of our sight and our messages would likely just litter someone's lawn. But for that one brief moment, our spirits, like those balloons, soared heavenward.

Two days later, the principal came on the public address system during fourth period. He said there would be an emergency assembly in the cafeteria at the beginning of fifth period. Even over the PA system, it sounded like he was crying.

We filed into that cafeteria in silence. No one wanted to guess what the principal was going to speak about. Everyone was nervous; some of the girls were crying. The principal stepped up to the podium and adjusted the microphone. He took off his glasses and wiped his eyes. Then he cleared his throat and began to read from a sheet of paper.

Dear Students of Archwood High School:

Today was the day I planned to kill myself. I knew exactly how I would do it, too. I planned to go into my garage, turn my car on and leave my garage door closed. You see, I had no reason to live. My only son was killed in a car accident a month ago. My wife died last year. The way the world is going, I felt that I would be better off dead. But when I went out to my garage, I found a red balloon stuck to one of the bushes in the hedge. It struck me as odd seeing that red balloon there against the bare branches of the bush. It seemed so bright and cheery. I didn't want to see anything bright and cheery so I went over to untangle it and throw it away. But it popped when I touched it and a piece of paper floated out. I picked it up and read it. That paper made me decide not to take my own life. Your message of hope touched at least one person today—one person who wouldn't be here writing this if I hadn't had a message that there are kids like you who care. Just knowing that you are in this world makes it a better place. Thank you.

For just a moment, the room was silent except for a few sniffs. Then a roar went up as the whole student body got to its feet, clapping and cheering.

It was as if those balloons had floated right up to God and He had guided them to someone who needed a message of hope. What began as a way just to make ourselves feel better turned out to be a miracle that saved the life of at least one man who would forever be a stranger to all of us. But how many other people's lives would our messages touch? Everyone wants to believe that he can make a difference in the world. We had proof that we had done just that.

When the message is positive, somehow God sees that it gets to the right place. ⚹

*I've always known it was wrong. But I* just couldn't help myself. If I saw something pretty, I wanted it. It didn't matter what it was or how much it cost. If it sparkled or smelled nice or had a pretty wrapper, I took it. I've shoplifted soap, shampoo, perfume samples, notebooks, and jewelry. Rarely have I taken anything that was over $50. I really don't know why I did it. It wasn't because I couldn't afford things or even because I didn't have the money on me. Shoplifting was fun for me—fun and exciting.

The only problem I had was how I felt afterward. When the thrill had worn off, I felt dirty—dirty and ugly as if I had a physical mark on me or some kind of disgusting and unmentionable disease. But that feeling would go away eventually and I would crave the thrill again. It was a vicious cycle that I couldn't break. And I wanted to break it. I wanted to stop. But I couldn't. And I couldn't tell anyone about it because I had stolen so many things already that if anyone found out, I would probably go to jail for a million years.

My parents would kill me if they found out. They always expected me to be this perfect, sweet little girl. Get good grades, go to church, show respect for adults. That was me, all right. Only it was all an act. I wasn't their good little girl. I was a shoplifter!

But, I told myself, the stores really charge way too much for their stuff. They make tons of money on the things I do buy. So I felt entitled.

But then I heard the three little words that every shoplifter knows the store security guard will whisper in your ear when you are busted: "Come with me." I knew the day would come but I felt my heart drop into my stomach when it finally happened.

I had been in the store for only a few minutes. Some crop top blouses at the back of the store caught my eye. I had wanted one of them for a long time—ever since my mother allowed me to get my belly button pierced. I figured, what was the good of having a ring there if no one got to see it?

On my way toward the rack, I passed the jewelry counter. Hardly aware of what I was doing, I picked up a few things and dropped them into my purse.

I expected to see a big burly man in a dark suit. Instead I saw a beautiful young blond girl, not much older than I was. She took my elbow and marched me up to the store register. I was a little surprised since I expected to be taken into a back room somewhere.

But my surprise turned to shock when the girl said loudly, "Jennifer, I'm going to buy those earrings for you for a present but don't you think you have enough bracelets and lipsticks? Let's put those back. Show the lady the earrings now."

She had been paying closer attention to what I was stealing than I had been! When I opened my purse, there were exactly the items she had mentioned. Without knowing what was really happening, I took the items out and put them on the counter. The blonde girl said to the saleswoman, "These earrings will look great on my sister, won't they?" That was when I knew she wasn't store security! She was pretending to be my sister and paying for the earrings I had stolen. Then she actually handed them to me!

"Come on," she said then, "let's go get an ice cream." I was so shocked I just followed her out of the store.

"This was your last chance. Next time, you won't be so lucky. You won't be lucky at all. Trust me. I know." She never gave me a chance to say one word. She was entirely normal looking, cute even, but she was creepy. Her words sounded ominous: *Next time, you won't be lucky at all!*

That night I was watching TV, flipping through the channels. Normally I hate the news, but a special story just caught my attention and I left the TV on that channel. It was a gruesome story about the justice system in Iraq. A young man had been caught stealing bread or something and the punishment was having his hands cut off.

I felt my stomach drop to the floor. I said a hasty prayer of thanks that I lived in a country where stealing isn't punishable by maiming. I looked down at my hands—pretty, manicured. When I looked up at the TV again, the camera was focused on the man's stumps. I quickly flipped the channel.

I stayed away from the mall for two weeks. That was a long time for me. Shoplifting is like a sickness or an addiction. You really can't just stop. But my experience was enough to make me try to stop and the only way I could do that was not to even go to the mall to look around.

It was really hard to stay away. I went to school, tried to concentrate on my homework, saw my friends, and went to my after-school job at the local animal hospital. When my friends suggested hanging out at the mall, I had to come up with a really good excuse why I didn't want to. What used to be a fun, normal activity for me was now a source of anxiety. I knew I wasn't capable of just going to the stores and looking. I knew that, once there, I would steal.

But I just couldn't help myself. When my friend May called me at work to ask if I wanted to go to the mall that evening, I agreed.

But I never got the chance. While I was helping the doctor give a shot to a dog that afternoon, the dog suddenly whipped his head around and bit my hand. Now, I was used to handling the animals and while all of us have been nipped here and there, very few of us have ever been bitten hard enough to break the skin. This bite required me to go to the emergency room, where I spent the better part of my evening. My mom told me she felt sorry for me but I was lucky it hadn't been worse.

The next time May asked me if I wanted to go to the mall, I was putting the dishes into the dishwasher. I cradled the phone on my shoulder and reached for the dirty glasses. Just as I was telling May that I would meet her at the entrance to Bloomingdale's, the phone slid out of my grasp and crashed down into the dishwasher, shattering all the glasses! I pulled my hand away, but not in time to avoid being cut. While it wasn't deep enough to require stitches, it hurt like anything. I couldn't go to the mall.

It wasn't until my third "accident" that involved my hand that I finally got the message. This time, I got as far as the mall parking lot. As I got out of the car, I pressed the automatic door lock and then proceeded to close the door on my fingers. It was all I could do to get my key back out and unlock the door. I wiggled my fingers to see if I had broken any. I hadn't but it smarted! I got back in my car and drove home with tears in my eyes.

As I pulled into the driveway, I wondered about my three "accidents." They all happened within a short time period, all when I was contemplating going shopping, and all involved my hands. Perhaps I was being given a message about how I should and shouldn't be using them!

Nothing happens by accident, I decided. I was being given a clear message: Stop shoplifting!

I stayed away from the mall for a month and nothing bad happened to me. During that time, I read a little more and my grades picked up. As a reward, my mother took me for a manicure.

And there she was. The manicurist was my pretty blond "sister" who had warned me away from my dangerous habit. She smiled up at me but gave no sign of recognition. Only after I sat down did she lean over to me and whisper, "Nice hands!"

That was all she said. "Thanks," I answered. "I think I'll keep them!"

I can't be sure, but I think she winked at me as I left. ✳

My grandmother Tess has twelve grandchildren and I am number nine. Each time a grandchild was born, Grandma made them a baby quilt. The quilts were all different. They were made up of any combination of colors: pastels and brights, and shapes: geometric as well as stars, moons, suns, or animals. I heard my grandmother say more than once that each quilt was as unique as the grandchild for whom she made it.

I guess I was about five when I first became aware that I was the only grandchild who did not have a handmade "Grandma" quilt. But I was about twelve when I realized it bothered me. Then I was sitting on my cousin Lainie's bed watching her pack for college. She carefully took the baby quilt off the wall where it had hung for as long as I could remember, folded it, and added it to her huge duffel bag. She told me that even if her roommate thought she was weird, she was taking her quilt because it reminded her of home, of Grandma, of her room, of everything that was comforting. And she said going off to college was hard enough without leaving behind every remnant of your childhood.

That's when I decided to ask Grandma why she had never made me a quilt. One evening, when she and two of my uncles and their kids were over, I asked her. She seemed surprised. "Of course I made you one! Didn't I? Oh, could I have forgotten you?"

"Don't you remember, Ma?" asked my Uncle Charlie. "Katy was born around the same time that Les got married and Tricia got engaged." (He was referring to my uncle and aunt.) "Maybe you were so busy with two weddings that you just forgot."

"Well if I did, I'll certainly fix that! Katy, I'm so sorry!"

My grandmother looked so upset, I hurried over to hug her and tell her, "It's all right, Gram. I know I'm really your favorite grandchild!" That was an old joke—every one of my grandmother's grandchildren considered himself or herself the favorite. We'd often tease each other—"I called Gram five times this week. She likes me best!" I'd tell my cousin Beth. Or "Gram and I are going out to lunch this week because I'm her favorite grandchild!" my sister Stephanie would say. The truth was that all of us adored her, and she made each of us feel that we were her favorite.

I thought I'd get one for Christmas or my birthday. But they came and went and Gram didn't say anything about the quilt. My mother asked me not to mention it anymore. "Gram is finding it harder and harder to use her hands these days. And she doesn't see as well as she used to. I know she wants to make a quilt for you, Katy, but please don't ask her again. It makes her feel bad that she can't do the things she used to."

I felt terrible. Of course it wasn't so important to me to have a quilt from my grandmother if making it wasn't fun and pleasurable for her to do it. My grandmother gave me far more important things than a blanket.

I thought about all the times I'd run to tell Gram about some important milestone in my life—the first time I lost a tooth, when I won the Science Fair, when I got my period, the first time a boy kissed me. Some of those things I had confided in my sisters and some of them I had told my mother. But I had told Gram everything.

Gram always had good advice for me and enjoyed my accomplishments. I could always count on her to read my mood and react accordingly. She never said, "Don't worry, you'll have another boyfriend," when my heart had been broken. (That was what my mother would say.) Gram would say something like, "That stinks! His loss, though." And somehow that made me feel better.

I thought about how my grandmother had reacted when I told her I wanted to be class president but I was afraid to run because if I didn't get any votes at all I would be embarrassed. She said, "If you don't run, you definitely won't get any votes at all." I ran and lost and ate ice cream at her house afterward. The following day, I went back to school and, fortified by all that ice cream, held my head up high. My grandmother had made it clear that I was still the same wonderful, worthy Katy whether or not I was class president.

"Tell her," said my mother when I told her what I was thinking.

I went over after school. She wasn't the homemade-cookies-and-milk kind of grandmother. She was more the let's-order-in-

Chinese-food-for-dinner type. That suited me fine. I told my grandmother a lot about my life over Cantonese.

On this particular day, I told my grandmother how much I loved her, how I felt she was always there for me, how I really always felt that I was her favorite. I didn't mention the quilt.

She brought it up. "I know you don't need a quilt to tell you I love you. But I want you to have something to remember me by when the time comes." That sounded ominous but she reassured me, "Oh I don't plan to go anywhere for a long time, yet. But you're not a baby anymore so a baby quilt seems silly. I'll have to think of something else." She hugged me an extra-long time when I left that day.

I didn't think about the quilt or our conversation that day until almost two years later. It was the day my eighty-nine-year-old-in-perfect-health-Chinese-food-eating Gram died of a stroke in her living room.

She left five children, twelve grandchildren (two more on the way), and a lot of friends to mourn her. It was as if a special chapter in my life was over. My grandmother had filled places in me that no one else had.

My heart hurt. I cried a lot and so did my sisters. I felt an especial pang, though, when I went into Stephanie's room and found her holding her quilt from Gram up against her cheek. That was the first time in two and a half years that I thought about the fact that I was the only grandchild without a quilt. Now was the time I really wanted one.

What I really wanted was something to comfort me. What I

really wanted was for my grandmother not to have died. What I really wanted was for things to stay the same and for my grandmother to still be there when I went over for Chinese food and good advice.

I went to her apartment with my mother and two of my aunts a week later. We intended to pack up everything—all her clothes and dishes, pots and pans, and silver. I wasn't much help to the grown-ups who were packing. I walked around the apartment touching things, trying to make her come back to me in my mind. I pictured us sitting at her kitchen table, saw myself using her spoons and dishes. It wasn't comforting. It just made me sadder and sadder. It made me think of all the years to come when I would be having experiences and she wouldn't be here to share them with—relationships with boys, friends, high school graduation, my wedding. . .

"Oh, Gram," I sighed to myself. "I'll miss you so much."

And then for some reason I'll never know, I went into her bedroom and opened the closet door. I expected to find it full of her clothes—ones that my aunts and my mother would take off the hangers and fold neatly to give away to charity. Instead the closet was half-empty. At the bottom of it was a box with my name on it.

"Mom! Aunt Trish!" I called. "Come see!" I waited until they were in the room with me before I opened it. Inside was a blanket—not a quilt exactly, but a hodgepodge kind of blanket. It was made up of different fabrics and patterns the way a quilt would be, but this one was definitely not for a baby.

This quilt had velvet and lace and satin in it—it took us all a moment to realize what we were holding. Then my Aunt Trish said softly, "This was from Mom's blue velvet robe. I remember seeing her in it when I was a little girl."

My mother fingered the white satin. "This is from her wedding dress. None of her daughters wanted to wear it but she couldn't bear to give it away."

I heard them all identifying each swatch of material: "This is from her red suit—you know the one she wore to Les's wedding!" "This is from her green wool coat—she wore that at Debra's graduation!" And so on. I didn't hear where all the pieces came from. I had stopped listening to their voices.

I was hearing another voice. Her voice. My beloved grandmother, telling me that I was never the forgotten grandchild. It smelled like her (and some of the pieces smelled a little like Chinese food). I pictured myself wrapped up in it, saw myself laying it across my bed at home now and across the bed in my college dorm room later and then on my bed in my own home after I was married. Whatever milestone was yet to come in my life, I would have Gram's quilt to remind me that she was there with me—as she always had been—loving me from wherever it was that God had taken her to.

The blanket had one square left unfinished. A note was pinned there. "For Kate to add on the day she realizes that love lasts forever. Love, Gram."

Denim would look perfect in the empty square. I was wearing blue jeans. ✳

During my senior year in high school, my parents were having a particularly rough time financially. My dad got laid off from his job and my mom wasn't able to work since she took care of my two younger siblings full-time. My brother, Daniel, has special needs, so my mom is always driving him to therapists and doctors.

When my mother's father died suddenly in November, my mother went to Arkansas to close up his house and settle all his financial matters.

My mother had never been especially close to her father, and she was an only child. I only saw my grandfather a few times in my life. I knew that there had been some sort of family quarrel when my parents got married. I guessed it might have been because my grandfather didn't like my dad. But through the years, no one ever told me. My mom hardly ever talked about him at all.

But every year on my birthday, my mother's father would send me a card with a check in it. The amount always equaled the number of years old I was. My mother would watch me as I wrote him a thank-you note. But that was all the correspondence I had with him. I admit I didn't love writing letters and since my mother didn't tell me to, I didn't try to communicate with this stranger. But he remembered my birthday in June every year.

All my life I dreamed of going to college. I wanted more than anything to become a nurse. When I was accepted to a nursing program at my first-choice school, I was ecstatic.

The only problem would be paying for it. I was offered a partial scholarship but it wouldn't be enough. I knew I could work but I worried that if I worked too many hours, I wouldn't be able to keep up my grades and the program I was going into was particularly competitive. More than nine students competed for each spot in that program. I had won one of them, but if I couldn't afford the tuition, I would lose it.

The deadline for all payments to be made to the school was July 31. As soon as I got my acceptance letter, I started working two jobs—one at a car wash, the other at a restaurant. My parents tried to be encouraging but my dad was already working two jobs and making less than he had before he was laid off. My mom was working part-time. Between the two of them, they were just barely making enough to support us and pay the mortgage. As school ended in June, I began to realize that I would have to face the fact that I wasn't going to college in the fall.

But somehow I couldn't bring myself to write that letter to the college telling them I didn't have the money. I kept putting it off. Oh well, I figured that when July 31 rolled around and they hadn't received payment, they would get the idea that I wasn't coming. It made me cry every time I thought about it.

I worked late every day during the summer and July 30, a Wednesday, was no exception. Everyone in my family was home, still up, when I walked in the door.

"There's a letter for you on the table," my mother said in a normal tone.

The first thing I noticed was the postmark. It was from Arkansas. The only person I had ever known from Arkansas was my grandfather, and the only time I ever heard from him was on my birthday, which had already passed. Of course I didn't get my card and check from him this year since he died six months before! And anyway, this letter was thicker than a birthday card and looked official—it had one of those little windows in the front.

It was from an insurance company. "Dear Lynn, You have been named as sole beneficiary of your grandfather's life insurance policy. . . ." There was a check inside for the *exact amount* of my first year's tuition and room and board at nursing college!

No one, not even my mother, had any idea that that check was coming. It was a gift from beyond the grave! Arriving just in the nick of time, it meant that I was on the way to fulfilling my dream of becoming a nurse.

I forgave him on the spot for missing my birthday by a month! ✳

*E*veryone knows you're not supposed to pick up hitchhikers. But when I went to Israel with my parents, I found out that the rules there are a little bit different.

The first thing I noticed, when we got out of the airport, was that everyone carried guns. There were soldiers with machine guns slung over their shoulders, and middle-aged men with pistols strapped around their waists. In America, carrying a gun on the street like that would get you arrested, but in Israel, it's a way of life.

As we started our two-hour drive to my cousins' house where we would be spending Passover, I saw a lot more guns. Every so often we'd pass a bus stop where soldiers were waiting to get home to their families for the holiday.

A lot of times, people who are driving by will stop and pick up a couple of soldiers and drive them to the next town, if they're going that way. In Israel, everyone serves in the army, so a soldier is always treated like family.

But I was sure that my father wouldn't stop and offer a ride to any of the soldiers. Our small rental car was already bulging with the three of us and our luggage. I didn't want to have to sit in the backseat next to some stranger. Especially one who was just a few years older than I, didn't speak English, and carried a gun.

After an hour, we reached the city of Netanya. My dad needed directions to Haifa, where our cousins lived. We had to arrive before sunset, when the Passover Seder would begin. We stopped at a large hotel.

My mother and I went to the ladies' room. I needed to freshen up. To my horror, I realized that I had packed my makeup, hairbrush, and even my toothbrush in my big suitcase, which was all the way at the bottom of the luggage piled in the trunk of the rental car.

When we came out of the ladies' room, I spotted my dad sitting on the other side of the lobby, talking to someone.

Wherever we go, he always manages to find someone, anyone, to talk to—sales clerks, bus drivers, even the custodian in my school. He asks them all kinds of questions about their jobs or their lives. It's really embarrassing. Once when I complained about it, he got really serious and told me, "It doesn't cost you anything to be friendly to people. And a lot of people are really interesting. But more important, you never know whose path you're meant to cross."

After that I didn't argue with him. I just put up with it. But this time, my dad was deep in conversation with an Israeli soldier, who was casually holding a machine gun across his lap. I looked at his face. He looked young.

My dad saw us and waved. The soldier stood up and put out his hand as my dad introduced us. His name was Leor, he told us, and he lived in Eilat.

Leor had a day's leave, but he had to be back at his army

base the next morning. There wasn't enough time for him to go home, since Eilat is about as far away from Netanya as you can get in Israel, so he had spent the day walking around the town. He didn't know anyone in Netanya, but he had heard that there was a communal Passover Seder at the hotel that evening, so he had come there to see if he could get a seat. This would be his first Seder away from his family.

I wasn't surprised when my dad said, "We're having a Seder at my cousins' house in Haifa. Please join us."

Before I knew it, there I was, squeezed into the backseat of the car with my backpack on my lap, having not had access to a toothbrush or deodorant for almost two full days, sitting next to an Israeli soldier. I was furious with my father. Now I would be expected to be polite and to make conversation with this stranger who was only three years older than I!

I barely knew any Hebrew, but Leor didn't seem to notice. His English was pretty good. He asked me about my school, how old I was, and whether I had been to Israel before. He seemed to be genuinely interested in my answers, and before long I found myself thinking he was funny and nice. By the time we got to our cousins' house, I wasn't angry at my dad anymore.

We unpacked and I helped Cousin Sarah set the table. There would be twenty-four of us at the Seder.

It was wonderful. Everyone took turns reading parts of the Haggadah out loud. We sang songs using the melodies that have been part of my father's family Seders for generations.

Suddenly, we heard people shouting in the street. "What's happening?" we asked, coming outside to join them.

A suicide bomber had blown himself up at a hotel. Many people had been killed, many more wounded. I saw Leor sit down heavily on the curb and put his head in his hands. "Are you okay?" I asked.

He raised his head and looked at me. "Can you understand what they are saying?"

"Not really," I admitted.

"The bomb was in Netanya," Leor said. "At the Park Hotel."

"The Park Hotel?" I repeated. That was the hotel where we had stopped earlier that day. That was where we had met Leor, and where my dad had invited him to come with us. And that was where he had planned to attend a Passover Seder that very evening!

"The bomber was disguised as a woman," Leor was saying. "He went right into the dining room, where they were having the Seder, and he blew the place up."

I felt cold all of a sudden, even though it was a hot night. I sat down on the curb next to Leor but I couldn't think of a single thing to say. This time it wasn't because I was too shy.

Eventually we went inside and resumed the Seder. Instead of laughter, singing, and joyous conversation, however, there was sorrow and prayer. Somehow, through it all, there was hope for the future. This surprised me a little but my relatives and Leor made me see that you really can't exist without hope—even in the face of this kind of awful tragedy.

It was well after midnight when we finished. The guests left, and the rest of us helped Cousin Sarah clear the table and clean up the kitchen. When we were done, Leor thanked Sarah and Ben for having him. He had to report to his base by 5 A.M., and the buses run infrequently during the night, so he had to leave right away.

My dad offered to walk Leor to the bus stop. He asked me to join them. It was late and most people were sleeping, so we were quiet as we walked.

We got to the bus stop with about ten minutes to spare. We sat down on the bench and looked at the stars and the brilliant full moon. Finally, Leor spoke.

"I don't really know how to thank you," he began.

"You don't need to thank me. It was my pleasure," my father answered quickly.

"No, but I do," Leor continued. "I don't know how, I can't explain it in English. And maybe not in Hebrew, either. But that was very special, what you did for me tonight."

My father didn't say anything for a few moments. Then he just said, "I guess it was."

We sat in silence, listening to the crickets, until the bus rumbled into view. Then Leor was gone, and the night was quiet again. My father and I turned and started to walk home.

I don't know what made me do it, but I took my father's hand as we walked. Was it a chance encounter, my dad picking Leor up like that? I thought so at the time, but as I walked back to my cousins' house with my dad, I knew differently. There, in that land of faith and miracles, I knew that my dad was an instrument in the miracle of saving at least one life. Somewhere in Jewish liturgy it says that if you save one life, it is as if you have saved the world. I stopped being embarrassed by my father then and started to be pretty proud of him.

Next time, though, when he saves the world, I'm going to be prepared and put my toothbrush in my pocket when I travel! ✳

*W*hen *I was six years old, my doctor* made a mistake that saved my life. My mother had taken me for my checkup for school. I would be entering first grade and all public schools required a certificate of health. It was early August 1992 and very hot in southern Florida where we live. But I remember getting to go out for ice cream after the doctor's visit because I had to have a shot and my mother felt sorry for me.

The state of Florida requires that children entering public school take a test for the presence of lead in the bloodstream. Some children who live in houses with lead-based paint have high levels of lead in their blood. Lead poisoning can cause mental retardation and even death.

On the morning of August 23, 1992, a Saturday, the phone rang. It was our pediatrician's office calling to tell my mother that I had dangerously high levels of lead in my blood. I would die without immediate medical treatment. And the only place to receive treatment was at the Children's Medical Center in St. Petersburg, several hours north of our home in southern Florida.

My dad was home from work that day. There had been warnings that Hurricane Andrew was headed our way, and my dad had stayed home to pile up sandbags and close our shutters. We had heard reports that the Keys were being evacuated, but since we were on the mainland, we never thought about evacuating. When the doctor called, my parents became so worried about me that they forgot about Hurricane Andrew. My parents must have been really worried about me because it was quickly decided that they would both make the trip. Of course, this meant taking my brothers, too. On the way, my mom played tape after tape of silly songs to keep me from being scared.

When we got to the hospital, I was admitted to the pediatrics ward and my parents were told that some additional tests were needed. My family was allowed to stay with me the whole time.

It took a long time to get the test results, and I watched a lot of videos on the TV in the lounge. My mom nursed the babies and my dad went out for food occasionally, bringing back whatever I asked for.

I remember clearly the doctor coming in around dinnertime with a peculiar look on his face. He said he would keep me there for the night, because the blood screen again showed no lead at all in my system. "One of us has made a mistake—either your doctor or me. I want to run it again to be sure. Also if our test is wrong, we can watch Todd for any signs of illness."

Then as he was about to leave, the doctor turned to my dad and said, "You've had videos on the TV all day so I guess you haven't seen the news. Hurricane Andrew is headed straight for the coast!"

On August 24, 1992, in the early morning, Hurricane Andrew hit the south Florida coastline, destroying everything in its wake. Many people were killed and several hundred thousand were left homeless, including us. Our home was completely destroyed. Nothing was left standing and everything inside was a total loss—my toys and our family photo albums. All of our possessions—all gone!

But our entire family was safe and sound in the Children's Hospital Medical Center in St. Petersburg.

It turned out my pediatrician was the one who had made the mistake. My blood levels were perfectly normal—not a drop of lead in me at all.

But the next time we saw him, we thanked him just the same! ✳

*I* have always loved music. I've played both the piano and the guitar ever since I was old enough to reach the pedals on one and get my fingers around the neck of the other. I also sing. When I was younger, I sang soprano in our church choir. As I got older and my voice changed, I sang tenor.

I love singing in the choir—both at school and at church. Our school choir actually has a national reputation and we have been invited to sing at the White House, at Fourth of July celebrations all over the country, and at special dedications, like a special performance for the workers cleaning up at Ground Zero.

I come from a musical family. Everyone plays some instrument. My grandmother is the only one with no musical ability. She claims to be tone-deaf. But she loves to listen to the rest of us. She loves to hear me sing anything, even rock music, because she says it is obvious that I love it. She's right.

When my grandfather was younger, everyone says, he had a very powerful tenor. My grandfather says I am on my way to being almost as good as he was.

Which is not to say that he never criticizes! On the contrary. After every performance, my grandfather has a list of suggestions for ways for me to improve. "Sing from your soul, boy," he says to me. "Remember, you have a special talent! Use it. When you sing, you have the chance to really touch people. Give them an important message!"

My grandfather has always encouraged me. "If music is your life, work at it and you'll be singing at Carnegie Hall someday!"

Until the National Choir Competitions, I didn't know what Carnegie Hall was. Then I found out that it is a famous music hall in New York City.

The National Choir Competitions are held there in August once every four years for high school choirs. Many of the participants—mostly, the soloists—have won music scholarships to Juilliard, one of the most famous music schools in the country. Our school had never won a competition, but when we were invited to attend my junior year, everyone really thought we had a chance.

Our choir director assigned me a solo from *La Traviata,* my grandfather's favorite opera. Listening to me practice, he told me to put some meaning into the words. "But," I said, "how am I supposed to do that if I can't speak Italian?" He said there was power in the music far beyond the words.

I found out exactly what he meant when my grandmother died two days before our choir was scheduled to fly to New York.

Of course I would sing at her funeral, which was scheduled for the same day and exactly the same time that our choir would be singing in Carnegie Hall. As disappointed as I was to miss the Nationals and singing at Carnegie Hall, it paled in comparison to the loss I felt for myself, but also for my grandfather.

There were no words to comfort him, I knew. But there was music.

I chose two pieces to sing. One was the "Gran Dio" aria from *La Traviata*. It's what Alfredo sings to his dying love, Violetta, to tell her how much he will miss her and how he will never forget her, and is in Italian. My grandfather would want to say those words to my grandmother and I could be his voice. I also chose one of my grandmother's and my favorite hymns—"Take My Hand, I Will Follow."

The pastor gave me the signal to move to the microphone after my grandmother's casket was brought down the long aisle of the church. I looked at my grandfather in the first row, at my parents, and at all the family and friends who had come to say good-bye to a very great lady. And I sang her to heaven.

For the first time in my life, I truly understood what my grandfather meant when he said, "Sing from your soul, boy!"

My voice filled the church. I closed my eyes and curled my tenor around every pure note of the aria. I may not have understood every word but I could convey their meaning: I sang words of love and undying devotion, a message that not even death could dim. When I finished, I looked at my grandfather. He looked up at me, dry-eyed and smiling! Then he closed his eyes and bent his head as I started my second selection, the hymn from me to my grandmother.

I noticed that the back door to the church was opened. The

day was cool and the church was crowded. I assumed the usher had opened it to let some air in. But as I sang, I saw a man come into the church. Slowly, he made his way down the center aisle. I wondered why a latecomer would come down the center aisle like that in the middle of the service, but then I noticed his cane that he swept across the aisle in front of him as he walked. He was blind.

I saw him pause halfway down the aisle and saw his mouth moving, saying the words of the hymn along with me, *"Take my hand, Lord. I'll trust in you. Lead me. Lead me. I will follow with perfect faith. And love."* Then I closed my eyes again to feel the rapture of the music. I felt a connection between my grandmother and me. When I opened my eyes, I did not see the blind man, but as I looked out at the sea of faces before me, I had the sense that they felt what I felt, not just loss but joy. My grandfather was right. There is power in music far beyond the words.

I didn't see the blind man at the burial or at the house later. But the following Sunday when I went to church with my family, I saw him dressed in a choir robe at the side of the church. He was leading our choir. Instead of a cane, he held a baton.

The pastor stopped me on the way out of church. "Emmet," he said, "I think you will want to meet the new choir director. He has something very important to say to you!"

His name was Mr. Rossini. He had lost his sight three years earlier from an eye disease. "A lot of people can adapt to being blind, but for me it was a death sentence. I felt panicky, trapped in everlasting darkness. I was afraid to go anywhere or do anything. I sat at home by myself most of the time. When friends came by, I'd visit with them for a while but I thought they just felt sorry for me so I asked them to leave. I lost my job and took disability pay. I thought about killing myself but I was too much of a coward. In three years, I haven't set foot inside any church, much less this one.

"But for some reason, I'll never understand, on the day of your grandmother's funeral, I did decide to get out, to see if I could find my way to my daughter's house by myself. I was terrified, but that day, I just felt I had to try. I got on the bus okay but I made a mistake counting the number of stops to my daughter's house. I got off one stop too soon. It put me off in front of your church. The door was open and I heard the voice of an angel singing a hymn that spoke just to me. I remembered that hymn from when I was a boy. It called to me. *You* called to me. I heard all the love and hope in your voice and I followed the sound.

"I didn't know I was walking into a private funeral. I'm sorry for your loss but I am more grateful than I can express that your singing brought me in here. The pastor told me there was an opening for a new choir director and I got the job!

"I decided there is some life in me yet, some purpose for me on this earth. I can't help being blind but I guess I don't have to be invisible!"

When Mr. Rossini stopped speaking, a shudder went through me. I don't know why people you love have to die. (Though what my grandfather said later *was* a comfort: "It was her time.

Thank God there was no pain.") But if it did have to happen, at least it made it possible for me to sing words of hope and faith to a blind man in need of both.

I hadn't saved Mr. Rossini's life—only God gets to decide who lives and who dies and when. But I had helped him find a way to make his life joyful again and that, said my grandfather, is all we humans can do.

I loved to play instruments. I never imagined that one day, I would be one. ⚹

*I*'m a good driver and I always wear my seat belt. It was a promise I made my parents on the day I got my driver's license more than two years ago. But it almost cost me my life!

One Saturday night, I was driving to pick up my girlfriend who lived a few miles from me in a neighboring town. It's a rural area, pretty wooded and the houses are set back from the road. But I'd driven that route a zillion times and, besides, it wasn't even dark out.

Twilight, I've since learned, is exactly the time that most deer like to come out of the woods. When the huge stag with the antlers bounded up from the side of the road, directly into my path, I braked hard. For a fraction of a second, I was close enough to look directly into its eyes. I pulled the wheel hard to the left to avoid hitting him. I missed him but my car careened down an embankment and slammed into a tree. I remember smelling gasoline and struggling to open my seat belt to free myself before my car burst into flames. To my horror, the seat belt jammed. I had one horrible moment of panic before I blacked out entirely.

When I came to, I was lying by the side of the road. I couldn't see anything clearly but I could smell the smoke from my burning car and I could hear the siren of the approaching ambulance and fire engines. Then I heard a voice above me say, "Just lie still, son. You're going to be okay." The voice belonged to the man who saved my life.

I found out later that Mr. Sherrick lived in the area and was returning home from work when he saw my car go off the road. He could have just called 911 on his cell phone, but he realized that there wasn't enough time for that. My car was going to go up in flames and I was trapped.

What he told me next convinced me that, without a doubt, God was watching out for me that day. Normally, Mr. Sherrick drives his own car to work and then home again. That day, just as he was getting into it to drive it home, he discovered that the tie rod had broken. He called a tow truck to come and tow it into the shop. But it was Saturday and no one would get to look at it until Monday morning. Mr. Sherrick had asked his boss to let him borrow one of the company trucks for the weekend since he planned to visit his son in another town that Sunday. His boss had agreed, especially since Mr. Sherrick wasn't scheduled to work at all that Saturday. He had come in only to finish up something as a special favor to his boss. The truck Mr. Sherrick had borrowed had one tool lying across the flatbed. It was a box cutter. That was what Mr. Sherrick had grabbed as he raced down the embankment to help me.

"I don't know why I grabbed that thing," Mr. Sherrick told us all later. "Something just told me I'd need it." Mr. Sherrick had used the box cutter to cut my seat belt quickly so that he could drag me away from my car. Just as he got me to the top of the hill, my car blew up!

I had a concussion and I needed nineteen stitches to close the cut above my right eye. I hadn't been able to see right away after I came to because of all the blood running down my face. But the scar I will have is a small reminder that I've been blessed. Mr. Sherrick was right where I needed him and had just what was needed for him to save my life.

I'm going to continue to wear my seat belt and to drive cautiously because now, I have proof that even if my parents can't see me, someone else is watching! ✳

*hen I was a senior in high school,* many things happened. I was invited to the prom, I starred in the class play, I was accepted to college, and my brother Noah died. When he died, he left a hole in our family and in our hearts that will never be filled. Despite that, Noah also gave us all, especially my youngest sister, Devorah, reason to believe absolutely that miracles really do happen.

On February 4, 1997, two military helicopters collided in Israel, killing over seventy young men and women —Israeli soldiers. Noah was among the dead. He made the decision to live in Israel on his eighteenth birthday, with my parents' reluctant approval. Though they would miss him, they had always raised all of us to have a deep love for, and commitment to, Israel. Three months after Noah arrived in Israel, Noah joined the Israeli Army.

Losing a brother is a terrible shock, but losing a child is worse. I saw my parents suddenly become old. Our family had planned to visit Israel and see Noah in the summer. Instead, we went in February to bury him. When we came back to our community, we observed the traditional week of mourning. It's comforting to have your family and friends share your grief. So many people loved Noah! But the response of my youngest sister, Devorah, frightened me. During the whole week of mourning and for some time after, she didn't talk about Noah or his death. Not even once. She didn't cry.

While this was happening to my family in Chicago, a fourth-grade teacher, Mrs. Royce, at a school in Toronto, Canada, was devising an innovative way to teach her children geography. Mrs. Royce hand-stitched a sixteen-inch rag doll with a large blue backpack. Her students named the doll Daisy.

Mrs. Royce's idea was to send the doll around the world to reach as many fourth graders as possible. Teachers were asked to have their students write notes about themselves and place them in Daisy's backpack. Each child was to say what he or she liked to do, what he or she thought he or she was good at, and what a typical day was like at school. In addition, each child was to write a personal message for Daisy to convey to the children in Mrs. Royce's class. The mother of one of Mrs. Royce's students sent Daisy to her sister in Cleveland, Ohio. From there, through various means, Daisy traveled to fifteen different countries and many cities within each country.

Daisy visited public schools, private schools, and some Catholic parochial schools throughout Canada, the United States, Mexico, Israel, France, Poland, and Italy. Eventually, Daisy came into the hands of Sister Mary Ellen Coombe, a member of the Sisters of Sion, a Catholic religious order with offices all over the world, including one in Israel and one in Chicago. Sister Mary Ellen heads the Institute of Inter-religious Affairs in Chicago.

Sister Mary Ellen arranged for Daisy to be sent to Akiva Day School, the school my sister, Devorah, attends. Daisy arrived there sometime in the middle of March, just as the Jewish holiday of Passover was approaching.

One day, her teacher, Miss Levine, called and asked to speak with my mother. I was at home, as I often was that semester. I was a second-semester senior, already accepted into college, and my mother needed me at home. I was doing everything I could to console her but my heart ached, too.

When Miss Levine called, my mother was in her bedroom with the door closed. I asked Miss Levine if I could take a message. There was a long pause while I suppose Miss Levine weighed in her own mind whether or not I was old enough to relay the importance of her message. Then she told me how worried she was about my sister. Devorah had completely stopped participating in class. Since Noah's death, Devorah had just been spending her time quietly drawing pictures. Miss Levine was worried.

Then, Miss Levine told me about Daisy. Miss Levine thought that the project would be especially good for Devorah.

But, said Miss Levine, Devorah had not turned in her assignment and the doll was scheduled to be returned to Canada the next day.

My hands grew icy and I heard a roar in my ears as if I were standing on a cliff overlooking the Red Sea as it parted. I will never know what kept that telephone in my hands. Maybe we all had Passover on our minds, but I knew without a doubt that another miracle was occurring and it was happening right there in our living room.

I knew about this project, but not from Miss Levine. Where had I heard about it? Oh, I knew! I screamed for Miss Levine to hold on; then I screamed for my mother to pick up the phone in her room. My hysteria must have frightened them both.

Noah had told us about that doll named Daisy! The day before he died, we had talked to Noah by phone, as usual. He had told us what he was doing and talked about his buddies in the army. He casually mentioned that one of his friends, a boy we all knew from Chicago, had opened a package from an acquaintance and taken out a funny-looking rag doll. He had passed it around when he read the message attached to the doll, and he had asked if anyone wanted to write anything to put in its backpack. Noah had held that doll in his hands. He told us that he started to write a note saying that he was in Israel, that he loved being there, where he belonged . . . but he hadn't had time to finish the note because his unit was going on maneuvers. He had given it back to his friend who repacked it and sent it back to his sister, Batsheva, a fifth-grader at Akiva Day School.

Noah had held that doll in his hands just before he boarded that helicopter. Daisy was the last thing Noah had touched before he died! And the only part of his message that he had had time to write was, "I love being here, where I belong . . ."

But Devorah had not been home when Noah called. Devorah hadn't had the chance to say good-bye. She never got to hear Noah tell her, as he always did when he called, how much he missed her and was thinking of her.

*And that he was where he belonged, that he was happy!*

My mother's face went white as perfect comprehension came over her. "Oh, God! Oh, God!" she cried.

Exactly, I thought.

Then we both remembered poor Miss Levine on the other end of the phone. My mother calmed down, took a breath, and started to explain to Miss Levine. But she didn't get halfway through her explanation when Miss Levine got it. Miss Levine told us to stay on the line while she went to get Devorah to the phone.

I heard my mother tell Devorah that the Daisy doll had visited Noah's army unit. I heard her tell Devorah everything. Then I heard my little sister tell our mother, "Noah did send me a message, Mommy. He just didn't put it into words I could hear."

I thought, But he did put it into words you could feel . . . we all felt . . . in our hearts.

The doll was sent back to Mrs. Royce in Toronto. Miss Levine told her about Devorah and Noah. Miss Levine thought that Mrs. Royce's class should know how they had participated in the most amazing miracle.

What began as a creative way to teach geography became much more important to everyone. It became a lesson in faith—proof that somehow God takes care of all of us. We don't know why Noah died in that crash. But we do know that

Teen Miracles ⟮ℰ⟯ 141

he had wanted to be in Israel ever since he was old enough to have an opinion. And we know that he loved us all, especially Devorah. He couldn't leave without saying good-bye to her and without telling us all that he was resting in the place he belonged in. My brother sent his message through a sixteen-inch rag doll.

The adults who heard this story were amazed. But the children weren't really that surprised. The message of love—brother to sister, God to all of us—was just one more thing that children, being children, just naturally knew all along.

*Names were changed to protect privacy. ✳

*T*he summer after I turned eight, my mom and dad took me, my little sister, and my brother to Disney World. I still remember the thrill of the roller coaster ride, holding tight to my dad's hand, the fun of seeing Mickey Mouse and Snow White, and how wet we got on the log run ride. At night, after we got back to our hotel, my parents let Tanya and me stay up late, watching TV in our suite and eating ice cream. We did some other fun things that summer, too. My mother took all three of us to the museums, beaches, and zoos in and around our home of Chicago. Sometimes, we packed a lunch and took a picnic to the park.

It was really the best summer of my life. I had no idea, at eight years old, that my mom had a premonition that she was critically ill.

It wasn't until we had started school again in September that my beautiful mother was diagnosed with leukemia. Leukemia is a form of blood cancer. Now that I am sixteen, I know more about the disease than most kids ever want to know.

On the day we got that call, my mother's blood counts were so bad that the doctors did not think that she would make it through the weekend, much less be cured.

But my parents were determined to make our lives seem

normal even while my mother was fighting for hers. We went to school, ate our meals—usually as a family—did our homework, and went to our after-school ballet class and music lessons. Sometimes my grandmother, a family friend, or my dad would take us. But we never missed anything.

At first, my mother stayed in the hospital for several weeks and we weren't allowed to visit. The risk of infection while being treated for leukemia is extremely high. The reason for this is that leukemia kills off the white blood cells that help the body fight infection. My mother received chemotherapy and blood transfusions constantly in the first few days. She didn't want us to visit when she was feeling so sick. But she asked us to keep journals of everything we did during the day so she could keep up with our lives. Tanya and I wrote about school, our friends, and how much we missed her and loved her. We drew beautiful second- and third-grader pictures for her that my dad brought to show her while he read her our misspelled words.

We didn't know it at the time, but our journals kept my mother alive. Her children were everything to her, and she resolved not to miss a moment of our lives. She was too sick to write back to us but we spoke to her on the phone and my dad brought messages and hugs and kisses from her to us. When she was able to have visitors, she made sure that the nurses disconnected her from all her tubes for the duration of our visits. She wanted to protect us from the reality of cancer and she wanted us to believe that she was our same Mommy who would soon come home. As children, we accepted that she was coming home just because she and my dad said so.

She did come home. For a while after the initial treatments, my mother had to go back to the hospital every day. But she arranged it so that she was home for dinner and to put us to bed and she was there when we woke up in the morning. After she got us off to school, she went back to the hospital, where she was hooked up to an IV full of chemicals. She spent eight hours a day at the hospital like that but made sure she was home in time for dinner. If keeping that kind of schedule was exhausting, my mother never showed it.

Being a mother was what she lived for, literally. Before she got sick, my mother talked often about another baby. But the doctors told her bluntly, "Be happy with the three you have and concentrate on staying alive for them for as long as you can. Don't even think about another baby." They told her that a complete recovery would take a miracle.

They had no idea that my mother would take those words to heart. She focused her whole being, not just on staying alive for the three of us, but on recovering completely so that she could give us another little brother or sister.

Another baby became her goal, her focus, as she fought her disease. Another baby would be her sign that God heard all her prayers and had cured her.

In Chicago, strangers of all faiths who heard that a young mother with three small children needed a miracle prayed for one for her.

I began to look for little signs that God was listening. And I began to see them. My mother had to be hospitalized in November and she stayed there for several weeks. We missed her terribly. But by then, we knew how important her treatments were. So we didn't pray that she would come home immediately. Instead, we set our goal on the Jewish holiday of Chanukah, which falls around Christmas. *Please, please*, Tanya and I asked God, *just let her come home to light candles with us.*

In my mind, the idea formed that if she could just make it home for Chanukah, she would make it home for good.

Chanukah lasts for eight days. In our family, we light a candle of the menorah each night and each of us gets a small gift. But I didn't want a small gift. I wanted a big one.

Seven nights came and went and the three of us lit our candles with my dad every night. With each passing day, I grew more and more fearful.

Then I came home from school on the eighth day, and there she was. She was standing at the door, waiting for us as if nothing was wrong. We lit the eighth and final candle all together. Nothing was ever more beautiful than the sight of my mother's smile in the glow of those eight flickering lights.

When children are taught about Jewish holidays, the word "miracle" is used only in reference to Chanukah. I wanted a miracle for my mother and I got it. She came home for Chanukah. When she went back into the hospital several weeks later, I wasn't afraid. I had been given a sign that she was going to make it.

That is how eight-year-olds think. No matter that the doctors gave my parents a poor prognosis. No matter that the tests showed only a small improvement in her blood count. No matter that she lost her hair and her strength. I knew, without a doubt, after Chanukah that she was going to live.

My birthday was in January and my party was scheduled for the very end of the month. Even though my mother had resumed treatment and was back in the hospital, I knew she would make it to my party. I'm sure the adults around me at the time meant well, meant to prepare me in case it was not to be. But I wouldn't listen. I just knew my mother would make it to my ninth birthday party.

She did. And she beat all the odds. But the real proof came on September 16, 2000. Exactly six years to the day that my mother walked into the hospital for her first chemotherapy treatment, she walked into the hospital again. This time it was to give birth to my baby sister, Nicole.

My mother tried to tell my sister and brother and me that she considered all her children to be miracles, gifts from God. I think she didn't want us to be jealous. But I'm the oldest and while I wasn't in the slightest bit jealous, I knew that my mother was just making that stuff up. Big sisters usually view new babies as playthings. Or as small annoyances who need to be baby-sat. But there was no doubt in my mind what Nicole really is. She is real, live proof that God listens. ⸙

*My parents have never made a secret of* the fact that my brother and I are adopted. But I never felt the need to look for my birth parents since I considered the parents who raised me to be my "real" parents. They loved me, took care of me, and now they are preparing to send me to college.

My mother did tell me when I was nine or ten that I could see a medical history if I ever needed it. It was information provided by the adoption agency that told my parents that neither of my birth parents had any genetic disease in their families. The letter from the adoption agency also told me that my parents were only teenagers when I was born, so that pretty much gave me the reason they had given me up. That was all the information my parents and I ever needed to know. As far as I was concerned, my life was complete.

That was why I was so surprised when, about a month before my eighteenth birthday, I was suddenly seized with the intense desire to know my birth mother's name and to communicate with her if I could. I had no idea where that feeling came from. I was perfectly content, about to graduate high school, had been accepted to college, and did not want to ever do anything that would cause my parents any pain.

I didn't tell my mother how I felt. I tried to ignore the feeling.

But a part of me wanted to be able to say to my birth mother, "Look at me today! I turned out pretty well, didn't I?" I wanted to thank her for giving me the chance to have such a good life.

I knew where my parents kept that letter with my medical history, and I looked at it to see the name of the agency. It was in upstate New York, a place we had moved away from when I was three.

I walked around with the name of the agency in my purse for a week before I finally went to the computer and searched for the agency's Web site. In less than a minute, I found it. But I logged off before I could bring myself to e-mail them. I went back to that computer a dozen times over the next two weeks, each time arguing with myself over whether or not I should contact them. And I never told my mother what I was up to.

On the day of my birthday, I woke up feeling excited and happy. My parents and my brother had planned a wonderful day for me and I knew they were excited to give me my presents. We gathered around the breakfast table and I opened them. I got a gift certificate for some clothes from my brother and a terrific laptop computer to take to college from my parents.

I set my laptop up on my desk and attached it to the modem. Without really thinking about it, I logged on and went immediately to the Web site whose address I had carried around in my pocket for a month. I scrolled down until I found the contact information. There was a list of seven counselors who received inquiries. I chose one name at random and clicked on the "write" icon.

"I am eighteen today and I was adopted from your agency at birth. I know that all records are sealed but I was wondering if any exceptions were ever made to reunite birth parents and their children? I do not want to cause any trouble for anyone. I was just interested in telling my birth mother that I am happy, have a good family, and am going to college in the fall. Would it be possible to let her know that? Could you tell her?" I signed my name and hesitated for a long minute before I hit the "send" key.

My family and I had a wonderful day. We went to the beach, did some shopping, and finally had dinner and a show in the city. It was a terrific way to spend my birthday and one of the last days our family would all be together before I left for college.

It was very late when I got home. As I prepared for bed, I went to my desk to shut down my computer for the night. But a feeling came over me and I just had to check my e-mail one time before I went to bed. I was almost afraid. Did I want a reply? What was I doing contacting the agency? Did I really want to find a woman who in all probability did not want to be found? Would the wonderful people who had just taken me out to celebrate the day I was born be hurt by my actions? Was I opening up a big can of worms?

I logged on quickly before I lost my nerve. I had a reply!

"It is the policy of this agency not to reveal any information about adoptions. There are no exceptions; otherwise birth parents and prospective parents would not use our services. We maintain their trust and consider it unethical, not to mention illegal, to reveal confidential information."

I was disappointed, though not surprised. I was about to log off when I heard those magic words, "You've got mail!" I quickly opened it.

"I put your address on my buddy list so I could see when you went back online. My sister was the one at the agency who answered your e-mail. She told me about you because she knows that for the past month, I have not been able to get you out of my mind. I am your birth mother. I wanted to wish you a happy birthday.

"The agency's policy is very strict. When I requested infor-mation about you about a month ago, they told me what my sister told you. If you had e-mailed anyone else, I would never have gotten your message. My sister would lose her job if anyone found out, so please don't tell anyone what she did. I am so happy to hear that you have had a good life. There isn't a day that goes by that I haven't prayed to God that you were happy. I can't be a part of your life but I want you to know that I will always love you. Thank you for sharing your birthday happiness with me."

There was no signature. I thought about pressing the "reply" button or saving her e-mail address. But I didn't. Instead I logged off and turned off my computer.

Message received. ⋇

*The day that terrorists flew two air-*planes into the World Trade Center in New York City is a day that no one will forget. The horror that came after the crashes as people first stared in disbelief, then ran for their lives as the buildings came down is something that no TV image could communicate. But I didn't watch it on TV. I was there. The high school I go to is at the south end of Manhattan.

The morning of September 11 was just like any other ordinary day. I slid into my seat as the bell rang at 8:30 A.M., the start of my English class.

I like English. I want to be a writer someday, and my teacher Mr. Beckworth is very encouraging. I had him the year before, my freshman year, and he taught me a lot about different kinds of writing.

We had been in session only about two weeks but Mr. Beckworth had already given a writing assignment. We had to write about a personal fear. The composition was supposed to tell how we developed the fear and what we might do to conquer it. I had no trouble coming up with a subject. I am deathly afraid of water and I know exactly why.

When I was three years old, my family took a day trip to the beach. It's not very far from our house and we have gone a

million times since the day I almost drowned. There wasn't anything dramatic about it. One minute I was standing on the sand, feeling it squish between my toes. The next minute, I was under the water, kicking my legs frantically, trying to find that safe, firm sand that I had been standing on a minute before. The saltwater burned my throat and I had time to feel abject terror before my older brother's hand grabbed my arm and pulled me to the surface.

He made fun of me for a while after that, imitating the way I came up sputtering and spitting. My mother wrapped me up in a big beach towel and carried me up the beach. I don't remember anything else about that day except that terrifying sensation of choking and breathing in seawater.

I knew my composition would be one of my best. I like writing personal narratives and I was looking forward to reading my essay aloud in class.

I never got the chance.

When the first plane hit, everyone thought it was an accident. The principal made an announcement over the PA system to stay calm even though he knew many of us had parents who worked in the WTC. Then the second plane hit.

We were told to evacuate the building. I followed my classmates into the hall and Mr. Beckworth turned off the lights. We were pretty orderly until we reached the doors. Then we heard a million sirens and everyone began to scream.

Day turned into night! It had been a sunny day; when the buildings fell, they created a swirling mass of black soot and dust so thick you couldn't see your hand in front of your face. My composition on fear had been about drowning; now I knew what real terror was!

No one knew where to run and pandemonium broke loose. Suddenly I felt a hand on my shoulder. I turned and could just make out Mr. Beckworth's face as he gave me a push, "Go that way!" he screamed.

I ran and ran. I couldn't see anything. There seemed to be thousands of people running with me. I didn't know where I was running; I only knew it meant death to stop.

And then I fell. It seemed almost as if I were falling in slow motion and I don't think my brain registered that two strong arms scooped me up, one on either side, and that two people were running with me in between them. I never saw their faces and my feet didn't touch the ground for at least a block. When they set me down, they said, "Keep going!" Then they turned and went back into the blackness. I could barely make out the yellow sleeves of their New York City fire department uniforms.

I did as I was told. I ran until I thought my lungs would burst. Then I stopped. I had nowhere to go. I realized that I had run south from my school away from the Towers. I was standing on the pier on the edge of the Hudson River! I knew that fire was coming up behind me but ahead of me was water. Only I couldn't see it. All I could see was hazy black dirt. Every fear I had ever had rose up inside my chest and I froze. I just froze. Nothing was going to make me jump into that river, but if I didn't, I knew I might be killed by all the falling debris.

Suddenly, I was swept into the air. I never felt a push . . . it was more like being lifted. I soared out over the water. That black, deep abyss of water—my personal terror! I couldn't see what was below me and I had a split second to imagine that I was falling into the icy fingers of certain death. But when I looked down, directly below me was a tugboat filled with people covered in that awful thick dust. Two men lifted up their arms to me. Somehow I landed, softly.

The tugboat sped across the river to the New Jersey shore. People in the town of Paulus Hook had come out to the pier with blankets. A lady wrapped me in one of them and guided me up the hill to a house on the wharf.

I learned later that people in tugboats, ferryboats, garbage scows, and any other type of boat that could carry people had snatched up a lot of children from the schools along the south end of the island. We were all transported to the New Jersey side. Most of the kids from my school were taken in by residents of the town of Paulus Hook, New Jersey. Many of us were dazed but few were hurt. We showered, borrowed clothes, and watched the horrifying images on TV. I suppose if we had wanted to, we could have stepped outside and just watched it all from the street in Paulus Hook. I didn't want to.

Cell phones and land lines didn't work for hours. I couldn't reach my parents to tell them I was safe until close to seven o'clock that night. My mother started screaming and crying when she heard my voice. My parents couldn't pick me up until the next day. New York was in chaos, and transportation was impossible. But my family and I were safe.

I remember everything so vividly. Living through an experience like this etches it in your head for the rest of your life.

What I couldn't remember and, I think, never will, was the face of the person who made me leave that pier at the edge of the Hudson River. I believe He has no human face. God lifted me as gently as if on a breeze or on the wings of an angel and deposited me in that tugboat. I couldn't do it, just couldn't force myself to jump blindly into the water. I couldn't have done it to save my life.

Like many teenagers, I just needed a push in the right direction. ✳

*Everyone always says I look like my* Grandmother Anne. She's my mother's mother and even I see the resemblance. We both have the same thick, dark hair (mine is natural, hers isn't anymore), the same green eyes, and the same heart-shaped mouth. Yes, I owe my grandmother my looks. I also owe her my life.

I have always been close to Grandma Anne. She used to live near us in New York City; now she lives in Florida, but my three younger sisters and I talk to Grandma Anne on the phone at least once a week. She always wants to know what's going on in our lives.

I always confided things to my grandmother that I wouldn't and couldn't tell my mother, my sisters, or even my best friend. Junior year was a terrible year for me. I fought all the time with my mother. Everything she did made me angry. If I was out with friends, she'd make me call home every few hours. She was always on me about homework, too, and about spending too much time with my boyfriend.

My grandmother always listened to me. She always let me give my point of view and she never judged me.

Once, when things between my mother and me got particularly bad, I asked my grandmother how it could be that she

understood me so well and my mother didn't have a clue. She told me that I was just like her when she was my age. But things were much different then, she said. Her parents were very strict and she was never allowed to voice her own opinion to them. She said that made her very angry, so she understands how I feel.

My grandmother's parents were killed in the Holocaust. My grandmother, herself, was in the concentration camps when she was a girl. She was nineteen when the war ended. I don't know much about her life as a girl or as a teenager. She never talks about her experiences during the war.

Once I found an old picture of my grandmother taken before the war, the only picture of her from before she was married. I was struck by how pretty she was and pleased when everyone remarked that I looked just like her.

My senior year started out just as bad as my junior year had been. Like all my friends, I started applying to colleges. But I knew I wasn't going to get in to any of the schools that they were going to. I tried out for cheerleading and didn't make it. I didn't get a part in the school play, either. And I absolutely hated my mother! No matter what I did or didn't do, she'd get mad at me.

I felt like I wasn't good at anything and I hated everyone.

Then I discovered something I was good at. The girls at my school, like most girls our age, loved to talk about clothes and dieting. We all looked at the magazines of the skinny models in gorgeous clothes. We all wanted to be thin and beautiful. All my friends could get into college and have great boyfriends. I couldn't control the fact that the colleges didn't want me or that I didn't have a boyfriend. But better than anyone else, I could control what went into my mouth!

It began slowly, my obsession with eating or, rather, my obsession with not eating. It was easy to skip breakfast because I was always in a rush anyway. I would "forget" to take money for lunch and just grab an apple and a diet soda from home. I had to eat something for dinner though because my mother would have noticed if I had eaten nothing.

I was always a little plump, not fat, really, but when I began losing weight, I loved the attention I began to get. And I loved the clothes I was able to wear!

Then I began to like how I felt when I hadn't eaten anything for awhile. There's a kind of head rush. And I really began to like exercising! When I finished a really hard run, I understood what my science teacher said about beta endorphins making you feel high.

I watched the scale like a hawk. If the numbers went down, it was going to be a great day. If there was an increase, I'd starve for the whole day. When I bought my first pair of size four pants, I was thrilled.

As could be expected, my mother wasn't so thrilled. She started to make comments. I began to wear baggier clothes when I left the house so she wouldn't comment on my thinness.

Then I learned some other tricks of the trade. At dinner, I would help myself to a portion of food and keep up a lively conversation while I pushed the food around on my plate. I was always the first to jump up and clear the table so I could empty my plate in the garbage without being noticed. I don't know when I realized that I couldn't even look at food without getting a little sick. Nothing appealed to me. If my mother made my favorite roast chicken and mashed potatoes, it just seemed like mud on my plate.

When I got lightheaded in gym class, my teacher threatened to call my mother. I lied and told her I was just having a heavy period and I needed to lie down. In fact, my periods had stopped.

But I was in control—or so I thought. I had read about anorexia in health class, but I was smarter than those girls in the books. I wouldn't starve myself to the point of illness! I just liked how I looked, how I felt, and how everyone said nice things about me.

It was particularly cold in February of that year but my grandmother came to visit. I thought at first that was odd since she hated the cold weather and we had just visited her during our winter vacation. But as always, I was glad to see her.

Since I had last seen her in December, I had lost another ten pounds. When my grandmother saw me though, she hugged me like always and didn't say a word.

Grandma and I liked to go shopping together. Since I was little, it had always been our special thing to take the train into the city and shop at Macy's Department Store. Then we'd go out to eat at a great hamburger place close by. I didn't want to eat at that restaurant but when Grandma suggested a shopping trip, I was ready.

I loved trying on dresses but I didn't want my grandmother to see me until I had them on for the same reason that I always wore baggy clothes around my mother.

I had just slipped out of my sweatshirt and was about to pull a cute little black dress over my head when my grandmother opened the dressing room door. "Look what I found!" she started. "You'll look great. . . ." She never finished her sentence.

With the dress half on, I turned to face my grandmother, hugging the dress to hide my nakedness. I stared at her. There was a horrible look on her face. But her eyes didn't meet mine. She was looking right past me into the mirror at my back. A small cry escaped her and she leaned heavily on the doorjamb for support.

"Grandma . . ." I began. But she didn't even hear me. Then she said softly, "It's me."

We stayed like that for what seemed like a long time. Finally I lowered the dress and slipped back into my sweatshirt. My grandmother was no longer watching me. She had closed the dressing room door and was seated on the chair in the dressing room across the way.

"Why?" she said. "Why do you want to do that to yourself? You are me exactly at your age . . . the age I had to wear this." She rolled up her sleeve and showed me the bluish numbers tattooed on her right arm.

I had known they were there, of course. I felt awful. What could I say to her? I had done something horrible to her, caused her terrible pain! And I loved her more than anyone in the world.

Something bad had happened there in the department store, between her and me, and I was desperate to make it right. She was the one person in the world whose opinion I cared about, the one person who had never passed judgment on me, the one person who had loved me in spite of everything and anything I may have done to push her away. And now, I knew I had hurt her beyond words, beyond comprehension.

"To think that I fought to live through that horror, fought when all my family, everyone I loved, died, to think I should live to see you, my beautiful grandchild, my favorite, the one who is most like me, come to this! Why? Why?" My grandmother covered her face and cried. I touched her shoulder. "I don't know if I can forgive you. Now you really do look exactly like me when I was your age. And I tried so hard to forget."

My heart broke. Suddenly, I understood. It was a message that no one else had been able to get through to me. My thinness wasn't beautiful; it was sick. I looked like a concentration camp victim, like her sixty years ago. Now I knew why she never had any pictures taken of her until years after the war.

She began to talk to me, then. She told me about the war and about seeing her mother, sisters, and everyone she loved die. She told me that she never understood why or how she survived. She said survivors have a lot of guilt about why they were allowed the miracle of life when 6 million others weren't. She talked a long time and I didn't interrupt once. When she was done, I covered her hands with mine. She said, "I think the reason I was spared was so that I could have your mother and she could have you. I have always seen myself in you and I have thanked God. You were me without the damage of the war, without the scars."

That was the moment I knew how sick I was and how much I needed help.

When I entered the rehab hospital, I weighed less than ninety pounds. I am five feet five inches tall. If my grandmother had not reached me as she did, I would have been dead in six months. My grandmother survived a Holocaust by the grace of God and got a second chance at life. Her survival was, in every way, a miracle. I got a miracle, too, a second chance at life.

I won't say everything was great after that. It wasn't. But I did get help. I went away to a hospital for awhile, finishing my last few months of high school there. I learned how to eat again, how to control my eating without letting it control me.

Today, as I write this, I am a sophomore in college in Florida, near where my grandmother lives. I plan to do something important with my life, maybe be a counselor to kids like me with eating disorders. My grandmother said she didn't know why God saved her, a common sentiment among Holocaust survivors. But I know. She was saved so she could save me.

*L*ow-income housing usually consists of several high-rise buildings placed close together. They were built to house a lot of people on a small area of city acreage, specifically donated for the purpose. Once, those apartment buildings were probably beautiful. But not anymore. I grew up there.

Poor teenagers who live in the projects join gangs, and drugs and guns are a way of life. My experience was the norm. Until the day I witnessed a miracle.

There were a few playgrounds that the city had put up in and around the apartment buildings. But the equipment there was old and rusted and most mothers wouldn't let their kids play there anyway for fear that they would get caught in gang crossfire.

Nothing green grew anywhere around the buildings. It was all cement and asphalt except for some patchy areas between the buildings. No sun ever reached these narrow spaces. They were ugly, scraggly, and brown and because they were almost always in shadow, they attracted a lot of gang play—people doing drug deals or "arranging things." Certainly nothing good ever went down on these patches of ground.

Then a group of old ladies in one of the buildings got the idea to plant a garden between two of the buildings. A garden!

Everybody laughed at them. Including me and my friends. But those ladies did it anyway. They bought some seeds and went down and started raking and seeding the ground, just as if they were out in the country instead of in the middle of the city of Chicago. For several hours they raked and hoed and turned over nothing but rocks. But when they were done, they had put four different kinds of vegetable seeds into the little dirt that was there.

That was at the beginning of the summer, the usual time when gangs get "busy."

Of course nothing grew, though several of us looked for turnips or greens shooting up. When it began to look like the old ladies' garden wasn't going to amount to anything, it quickly became gang turf again.

That summer, several kids got killed, including a twelve-year-old whose brother vowed to avenge his killing. Word got around that this brother was out for blood. But the grand-mother of these two boys—the one who died and his brother—was one of the "Garden Ladies," as we had nicknamed them. She begged her grandson not to cause any more harm.

I know because I was standing next to my best friend when his grandma said it to him.

But he couldn't let it go. He put the word out that he wanted a meeting at nine o'clock that night. The meeting place was the space between the two high-rises. It was the perfect spot for a killing—too hard for police to get to quickly but easy enough for those who knew their way around the projects to get away. It couldn't be seen from the street and it was dark.

Our side approached from the north; the other gang approached from the south. Twelve gang members from our side showed up and I don't know how many showed up from the rival gang.

But not one shot was fired. When we got to the place, there was something between us:

It was a five-foot-tall white flower with a red center. It is the God's honest truth that it wasn't there the day before!

Two guys went up to touch it. I heard someone shout, "Madre Dio!" (Mother of God.) "It is real! It's got roots and everything!" A few of those tough guys went down on one knee and crossed themselves. But no one got hurt that night. Two bitter rival gangs with a score to settle couldn't bring themselves to settle it that night in that spot.

That flower bloomed all summer. As a matter of fact, it stood straight and tall well into November. As far as I know, nobody watered it and it never got any sunlight. It was probably a weed. But it was the most beautiful weed any of us had ever seen. Kids from both sides of the turf sneaked back there to take a look at it. And there was an unwritten rule among the gangs afterward that that place was sacred ground, off-limits for settling scores.

The projects are still ugly and dangerous. But for one summer, at least, there was one bright spot where something beautiful and worthwhile grew. If it happened once, it could happen again. ✳

*My dad and I were really close. It* wasn't just that we liked to do a lot of the same things like watching horror movies and going fishing. It was more than that. He was my best friend.

He never really yelled at me or lost his temper. If I did something wrong, like the time my friends and I got caught drinking at a party, he hardly even said anything. He just looked at me with those clear blue eyes, and I could see how hurt and disappointed he was.

He was always telling me that I was strong, and that I had a clear vision and would make good decisions in life. He said I had great "inner resources." "Listen to your inner resources," he always told me. "They won't steer you wrong."

He was a good listener. I could tell my dad anything and he would listen. He didn't always tell me what to do. Sometimes he didn't say anything at all. But after talking to him, I always felt better.

The best times were when we went fishing in Canada, where my dad grew up. We've gone every year since I was five years old. We spend a night or two with my dad's sister, and then my dad and I go off by ourselves and spend a week camping in the woods, catching fish and then cooking them over a campfire.

Last summer was the best trip yet, when my dad taught me to drive. I was only fourteen, too young for even a learner's permit. But my dad took me out into the country, on old abandoned dirt roads where you never saw another car. He just moved over into the passenger seat and gave me the keys. It was exciting, but it was harder than I had expected, and scary.

"Listen to your inner resources," my dad said again. "They won't steer you wrong."

But a week or two after we came back from Canada, my dad started to get sick. We found out he had cancer. It was a really bad kind, the kind that seems to appear suddenly and then grows really fast. They tried chemotherapy, but it didn't help. He knew he was dying, and he insisted we talk about it. He talked a lot about how strong I was, and how proud of me he was, and how I would have to take care of my mom and my little sister. He told me that my "inner resources" would carry me through the hard times.

He died in January. Just like that, he was gone.

For the first couple of weeks after the funeral, I was kind of numb. My friends came around, but they didn't really know what to say. My teachers tried to be really nice to me, too. They all told me to take as much time as I needed to get my work done. I think everyone expected me to grieve for a few weeks, then pull myself together and get on with my life.

I just couldn't seem to pull myself out of the dark fog. I went through the motions of going to school and hanging out with my friends. I tried to be cheerful and cooperative at home, so I wouldn't make things any harder for my mom than they already were. But I didn't really care about anything anymore. I didn't make up all of my schoolwork and when June came, I'd failed every class.

I was given the summer to make up my grades. But for the first week or so of summer vacation, I just hung around the house. My mom didn't make me look for a summer job because I was supposed to be working on my schoolwork. When she realized that that wasn't going to happen, she announced that she was sending me to Canada.

I was shocked. I couldn't understand why she wanted me to go. What was I supposed to do, go fishing by myself? But my mom insisted. Two days later, I was on a plane.

My aunt picked me up at the airport, and we drove out to her house. She lives in a little town about half an hour outside the city. There are lots of farms and lakes where you can go fishing. You can walk into town from her house. There's not much there, just a small grocery store, a drugstore, and a combination hardware store and bait shop.

After I had unpacked my suitcase, my aunt asked me to go into town and get some milk and eggs. I didn't mind at all. I was happy to go for a walk after sitting on the plane for three hours.

It was a hot day, and by the time I got to the store I was really thirsty. I bought the milk and eggs and a cold root beer for myself. The cashier asked me my name.

"Are you visiting someone here in town?" she asked me. I told her I was staying with my aunt, Carrie Winters.

"Oh, she's such a sweet person," the cashier said. "You tell her Velma says hi, okay?" I had the impression that this was a town where everyone knew everyone else.

Every day after that, my aunt sent me to town for something. I didn't mind. I liked going to the store every day, buying whatever my aunt needed, sitting on one of the benches outside the store and drinking my root beer. People were friendly and I could just be, without having to really think about anything.

I noticed that whenever I sat down in front of the store to drink my root beer, the same old man always sat on the other bench, a few feet away. He always had some kind of fishing equipment with him—lures or hooks or bait. Seeing that stuff reminded me of my dad and all our great fishing trips.

One day, the man got up and came over to me. He didn't introduce himself; he just started talking about his fishing lures. He had a lot of really nice ones, and we talked about them for a few minutes. Then he stood up.

"Well, I expect I'll see you tomorrow, Dan," he said, and headed off down the street. I was halfway home before I realized that the old man had known my name. I hadn't told him.

When I went back to the store the next morning, the old man was already there, in the same spot. I asked him how he had known my name.

He looked up at me, squinting into the morning sun. "This is a small town," he said finally. "You spend any time here, you'll see that people will know a whole lot more about you than just your name."

It became a regular routine: I bought whatever my aunt had sent me for, and then the old man and I sat on the bench while I drank my root beer and he repaired his fishing lures. We talked about fishing, mostly, and other things he knew about, like farming and sailing. His name was John Peters.

He never asked me anything about myself, or my school, or my family, or why I was spending the summer at my aunt's. And he especially didn't ask me about my dad. I figured he probably knew all about me, since it was a small town, like he said, and everyone seemed to know everyone's business. I'd had to talk to a lot of counselors after my dad died, and I was sick of talking about it. With John Peters, I could talk about anything I wanted. I felt comfortable with him.

The summer days seemed to go by quickly after that. The morning of my last day in Canada, I went into town as usual to talk to Mr. Peters.

"I'll sure miss you, Daniel," he told me. "It's been good talking with you in the mornings. You'll do fine, you know," he said. "You just listen to your inner resources, and you'll do fine."

That's what my dad used to say, I started to tell him. But by the time I looked up, he was already walking away, down the street. A truck came by just then, and when the dust cleared, Mr. Peters was already gone.

I left early the next morning. I'd made up all of my work over the summer, and that was a relief. It was good to see my friends, too. It was still hard a lot of the time, especially when I would wake up at night thinking about my dad. But as the months went by, the nightmares came less often.

It turned out to be a pretty good year, overall. My grades still weren't great, but I passed every class. I thought about getting a summer job. But what I really wanted was to go back to Canada.

My mom thought that was a good idea. I could get a job there, she said, and my aunt could always use my help. Less than a week after school ended, I was on a plane.

I arrived at my aunt's house in the evening. It was too late to go into town. I could hardly wait for morning, and as soon as it was light, I got dressed quickly and set off for town. I didn't even wait for my aunt to wake up so she could tell me what she needed from the store.

When I got there, the hardware store and the grocery store were just opening up. There were only a couple of people out, and I didn't see Mr. Peters. I sat down on the bench and waited. But Mr. Peters didn't come. Finally, when I couldn't stand it any longer, I went into the hardware store and found Ben, the owner.

"Well, hello there, Daniel," he said warmly. "You're back for the summer?"

"Yes," I answered, "I'm going to help my aunt, and maybe get a part-time job."

"Well, that sounds just fine," Ben said. "It's good to see you again. Can I get you something?"

I shook my head. "No, thanks," I answered. "I just came into town to see Mr. Peters. Has he been in here today?"

Ben looked at me. "Peters?" he said. "I don't recall any Peters. Who is he?"

I was completely surprised. "You know, Mr. Peters," I said. "John Peters. The old guy who always sits outside on the bench, with the fishing lures? I sat there with him every day last summer."

Ben scratched his head. "Peters . . . John Peters," he repeated.

"Sorry, Dan," he said. "Don't know him. Why don't you go next door and ask Velma? She knows everybody and everything that goes on in this town."

I went next door and asked Velma, but she said the same thing. No one had ever seen him. It was as if he had never existed.

I walked slowly back to my aunt's house, thinking about him and about my dad and about how well I had gotten through the year. I thought about how both Mr. Peters and my dad had told me to use my "inner resources."

When I got back to the house, my aunt was standing on the front porch.

"Good morning," she said. "I was surprised that you were out already when I got up. But I wasn't worried. I knew you'd be okay."

I was okay, I realized. Mr. Peters wasn't there, and my dad wasn't there, but I was okay.

"Did you get what you needed in town?" she asked.

And then because I knew it was true, I answered, "Yes, Aunt Carrie, I got what I needed. I got exactly what I needed in town."

*s I stood on the corner with my* friends, waiting for the light to change that day after school, I could hear the young couple behind us arguing. I couldn't make out what they said, but the words didn't matter. The fear and helplessness in the boy's voice told me he was trying to convince the girl to forgive him for something. The anger and hurt in her voice told me that she wasn't listening. That's when I felt that awful sense of terror . . . I had heard this kind of conversation before and I knew how it could end.

Four years earlier, I was living in St. Petersburg, Russia. I was thirteen years old. It is very cold in St. Petersburg. On a winter day that changed my life, it was twenty-nine degrees below zero. But we were used to the cold, so, as usual, my best friend and I walked from the bus to school, happily talking about normal things—school, boys, and movies we planned to see. It was still dark outside but we were in a good mood.

Lisa was an interesting girl. She could make everyone around her laugh or smile just by being near them. Everybody liked her. On a cold, dark Russian morning, Lisa's warmth attracted people and as we walked, we were soon joined by other friends.

At the end of school that day, I was standing outside with some of my friends, waiting for Lisa so we could go home together. Suddenly the door of the school flew open and Lisa ran out, right past my friends and me. We could see that she was crying. Then, her boyfriend, Mischa, ran out, calling her.

If any of us had thought fast, maybe things would not have turned out as they did. But all of us were too surprised to react. We all just stood there, rooted to the spot, surprised at seeing the two of them behave like this.

Mischa told me later what had caused the argument. He said he and Lisa had had a stupid fight. It had started as a joke— Mischa had said something that Lisa misunderstood. That's all it was, he said, a silly misunderstanding. It was normal.

But Lisa was hurt enough to run away from him—and from the rest of us. I called after her but she ignored me. Lisa ran blindly toward the corner of the boulevard that ran behind our school. She wasn't paying attention. That's the only explanation I can think of for what happened to her. She ran into the street, never even seeing the car that hit her.

My family moved to America later that year. Mischa had dropped out of school.

I had my own nightmares about Lisa's death. It is hard to see someone you know so well and love get killed and to know that even though you were right there, within a few steps, you couldn't have saved her. After we got to America, I often woke up in the middle of the night from a bad dream about the incident. It was scary.

But a part of me was very angry with Lisa. I couldn't understand why she did what she did. How could she have left us all—her mother, her boyfriend, me? How could she have wasted her beautiful self over something so stupid? If only she had stopped at the street and waited for Mischa to catch up to her and explain. Sometimes, my dreams would be so real, I would wake up crying. Then, when I tried to go back to sleep, I tried to imagine a different ending—one where Lisa stopped—and lived.

I suppose it is natural to wonder why such a thing would happen. No one ever had any good explanation for me—not my teachers, not my counselors, not my new friends here in America.


I liked my new high school and I made a lot of friends. There were other Russian-speaking kids there and I hung out with them a lot. But I made many friends who spoke only English, too, and my English quickly got better. (We had studied English in my school in Russia, so I could understand a little bit when I first arrived.)

Life here in America seemed very similar to my life in Russia. Until that moment on that street corner, four years later, I had no idea how similar.

My friends and I were waiting for the light to change when I heard them. The girl was very angry and crying. The boy kept trying to reason with her but she wasn't interested. I saw him touch her arm and I saw her pull her arm away and start to run! She came right toward my friends and me at the corner! Right toward us, running at top speed! Just as if she had no intention of stopping and waiting for the light!

No! I thought. Not again! Never again!

In America, I had learned, you don't get involved in other people's business, especially out on the street. None of my friends would have even thought to grab hold of the girl as she approached us. It just wouldn't have been their natural reaction.

But I did. I grabbed her jacket as she flew past me. I dropped my books all over the sidewalk and just grabbed the coat of a perfect stranger! She turned around, furious. But she stopped!

I didn't say anything to her. I didn't have to. Her boyfriend had reached us and he begged her to just listen. She tried to pull away from me. But I held on. When the light changed, I said to her, "Now you want to run? Go ahead. Nothing is worth getting killed over!"

She caught her breath. Then she said, "Oh! I didn't realize! I . . . thank you."

She was still angry at her boyfriend but she had calmed down enough to listen to him. I watched them walk away. Then, I crossed the street, but I continued to watch them talking for a little while. My friends and I continued down the street, our minds back on each other. I was halfway down the street when I heard a voice behind me yelling, "Wait, please! I don't even know your name!"

She was alone but she was running after us. I stopped and smiled at her.

"Hi," I said. "My name is Marina."

"Hi," she said back. "My name is Lisa."

My brother Jamie is not really my brother. He is my son. I was fifteen when he was born and my mother and I both wanted me to finish school. My mother and my grandmother take care of Jamie but neither of them loves him more than I do.

There were a lot of reasons I had Jamie. I wanted someone to love and who would love me. I had never been especially pretty and I know I'm not smart, so when I began to date Jorge and he told me how special I was, I believed him. He made me feel good about myself and I started to overlook my family's strong Catholic views. Jorge is not a bad guy and he comes over to visit Jamie every once in a while.

Jamie was always beautiful. Right from the start, he had thick black hair and big brown eyes that seemed to know me the second he was put into my arms.

For two years, everything was fine. I went to school and worked. My mother worked and my grandmother stayed home with Jamie. She always said he wasn't any trouble. I loved coming home to see him. My grandmother would keep him up late so that he could play with me a little when I got home from work.

But one day, Jamie got sick. He cried and cried. I stayed

home with him for a few days but I couldn't make him feel better. Neither could my mother or grandmother. We took him to the clinic. When the doctor there told me Jamie had to go to the hospital, I saw my mother cross herself and close her eyes. I knew it was bad.

Jamie's liver was sick. The doctors gave him all kinds of medicine—medicine that made him look so awful. His face swelled up so much that he could barely open his eyes. His beautiful, smooth skin became yellow. He didn't look like my Jamie anymore. And my sweet baby became so quiet. He slept so much.

My mother and my grandmother told me that Jamie might die.

I went to church. I asked God not to take away my baby.

Our church is a big place. It is located in the city and a lot of people go there. I don't know everybody. But it doesn't matter. When I go inside our church, I feel something powerful. I know that God listens to me there and that makes me as good as anybody else. I don't feel that way all the time when I'm not in the church—when I am in school, for example, or when I had to sit with Jamie in the hospital.

In school, it is hard for me and sometimes the teachers yell at me. Sometimes I don't understand everything or I don't finish my homework.

In the hospital, the doctors tried to tell me that I would lose Jamie. They said he needed a new liver and that it would be almost impossible to find him one. I offered to give him mine.

They said that I might be able to give him part of mine. But after they did some tests, they said Jamie and I didn't match. How could that be? I am his mother. His father had put too many bad things into his body to be tested—drugs and stuff.

Then the doctors told me it would be almost impossible for them to find someone to give Jamie a new liver. With a Hispanic mother and an African-American father, Jamie was different. And livers have to match exactly. Jamie would probably die, they said. I couldn't let that happen.

I asked God to save my baby. I asked Him every day. Even as I watched Jamie get sicker and sicker, I asked God.

One day when I went to the hospital, Jamie had been moved. He wasn't in with the children in the ward I was used to visiting. He was in a special place where each baby was in a separate room. Jamie was hooked up to so many machines that made different noises when I stood over his crib. Jamie made no noise.

A nice nurse held my hand. She said that Jamie wasn't in any pain and that I should just leave it in God's hands. I looked at her. She seemed young, not much older than I was. I told her that, of course Jamie was in God's hands. He always had been. I kissed my son and went home for a little rest.

In the middle of the night, the phone rang. The phone is in the hall, so my mother got to it before I did. She turned away from me as she spoke. Then all of a sudden she turned around and faced me with a big smile on her face.

"Get dressed, Maracita!" she said. "We have to go to the

hospital! Jamie is going to get a liver!"

We got to the hospital in time to kiss Jamie before they wheeled him into the operating room. A nurse came out and explained everything that was happening. A perfect match had been found for Jamie in the national organ registry from a baby who was also part Hispanic and part African-American and it was being flown in from Indiana, an hour away. She told us there was still a chance that Jamie would die.

My mother asked me if I understood. She knows I sometimes have trouble understanding a lot of things. Then she told me how grateful we should be to all the doctors and to the nurses who were going to save our baby.

I told her, "All the doctors know how to do is give medicine and take things out of some people and put them into other people. Then they tell you that what they do may or may not work. Can one of them make a flower or a single leaf on a tree? No! Only God can do that. I didn't ask the doctors to save him because I knew they couldn't. Only God could. I asked Him."

I may not be the smartest person in the world. I may not understand everything they teach in school or what these smart doctors have to say. But I understand that only God can bring miracles. I'm smart enough to know that.

And I'm going to teach that lesson to my son. And I'm going to teach him to pray as I will do every day of my life from now on for whoever it was who gave a perfectly matched liver to my now-perfectly healed son.

I stopped going to church the day my little boy died. He was only four and he didn't deserve to die. He was on his way with his daddy and his uncles to his grandmother's house in Indiana. They left late because his uncle couldn't get off work. Bobby was asleep in the backseat. Those men, they never even thought to tell Bobby to put his seat belt on! But they had them on, and that's why they all walked away from the accident with only scratches. But my Bobby had brain injuries. They took him to the hospital and kept him breathing until I could get there. But I could see the minute I looked at him that he was already gone.

I kissed him good-bye and told them they could turn off the machines.

Why did my baby have to die? I know I was too young to have him when I did but I took such good care of him. In our building, all the ladies loved him. They were all his "Grannies." And he was as friendly as anything. He smiled at everyone— even the drug dealers who hung out on the corner.

And Bobby loved school. The teachers there were even teaching him his letters and numbers. They said he was smart and that he loved to learn! Why did he have to die?

I didn't even have enough money to bury him properly. I had to borrow it from my aunt. I made all the arrangements to have Bobby brought home from the hospital in Indiana. His daddy tried to help me. But I didn't want his help. I didn't want to look at him even though I knew the accident wasn't his fault.

I came back to Chicago by myself. It took an extra day for Bobby to come home. The doctors in Indiana asked me if I wanted to donate any of Bobby's organs. The doctor who asked was really nice. He seemed sad when he told me that my Bobby had been so healthy in every way that maybe some other child could use his heart or his liver or his eyes.

Yes, I said. He was so healthy, wasn't he? I took good care of my baby. I signed the paper.

When I got home, it was close to dawn. I had to be at work at eight. I knew that my boss would let me off when I called but I didn't want to go home to sleep. So I went to church.

The church I grew up in, where my son went to school, is a big, beautiful building in the city of Chicago. I have known the priests there a long time. I always loved going inside that place. It seemed so peaceful. But that morning, I couldn't find any peace. Not in church, not in my head, and not in my heart. I tried to pray, to ask God to watch over my Bobby, but I couldn't find any words.

Why did life have to be so hard? Nobody ever gave me anything I didn't work hard to get. Not my mama or my daddy or even my boyfriend. About the only good thing I ever had in my life was my little boy. And I wanted his life to be different from mine. I wanted him to go to school, a good school, a safe school. He was going to finish high school—not like me—and stay out of the gangs and off drugs. He was gonna be somebody.

His daddy was trying to get himself together, too. He's really a good man. But sometimes things just push you so far down you can't pull yourself up very easily. Roberto was that way. But he loved me and I loved him and we had been a family in our own way. I didn't know if I would ever be able to forgive him. Or if he would ever forgive himself.

Roberto had been raised in the church like I was but he didn't go anymore. After Bobby died, I began to think Roberto had the right idea.

But habits are hard to break. So even though I was sure God wasn't listening to me anymore if He ever did, I continued to go to church.

But I couldn't pray.

Grief is a terrible thing. It hardens you.

I wouldn't let anybody comfort me. After Bobby's funeral and for weeks after, I just went through the motions of living. I'd go to work, come home, say a word to my aunt and my grandmother, maybe eat a bite, more often not, and go to bed. I didn't want to see my girlfriends; I didn't even want to go out with Roberto, which was just as well. He blamed himself for Bobby's death and even though I didn't think it was his fault . . . well, I just couldn't be with him the way we used to.

And I continued to go to church even though not one word of prayer came out of me.

Our church is big—it's the largest one of its kind in the city of Chicago. More than 10,000 people go there. One evening as I sat in one of the pews in the middle of that big empty space, I noticed a girl around my age at Mass. I think I had seen her there at other times as well but that particular evening, we were the only ones in the church and as big as it was and as empty, we both moved up to the front. She smiled at me. I guess she couldn't see that I didn't want to smile or talk or anything, because after a few minutes, she came over and sat down next to me.

Her English wasn't too good but she told me her name was Maracita and she was praying for her son. I think if she had said anything else I would just have given her the freeze and moved off. But that stopped me cold—that part about praying for her son.

"Did he die?" I asked. She seemed surprised. "No," she said. "He is alive, very much alive. But he was very, very sick. I asked God to heal him and he did."

"Lucky you," I said. And then I just burst into tears. I don't know where they came from—my toes probably, it felt so deep. But it was so unfair. Here I was grieving over my little dead boy and now this girl is here in my face telling me God saved her boy. Well why hadn't He saved mine? What was wrong with my Bobby or me that we didn't deserve a miracle?

The girl put her arms around me and for some reason, I let her.

And then I felt it. Later, when I told my momma about it, she told me her people down south would call what I experienced a "spell." But it wasn't a spell, as far as I was concerned. First, I felt a coldness in the room, then warmth, and some sort of movement. I can't describe it. And I felt it all at once. I started shaking so hard I thought my teeth would fall out. But this girl just kept a hold of me, like I was her friend or her child or something. She was kind of rocking me and she started humming. I didn't know her at all but something was happening all around me and somehow I knew I just had to stay where I was, locked tight in this girl's arms.

How long I stayed like that I don't know. I closed my eyes. And maybe because of all the crying and shaking, I fell asleep. When I opened my eyes, I was lying on the pew with my head in Maracita's lap. She looked down at me and smiled.

That was when I knew that there was something strange between her and me, something unexplainable.

"Your baby . . . ," I said, "What was wrong with him?"

"He had a bad liver. He got a new one. God gave him a new one, a perfect match." If I had ever been a person of faith in my life, her next words brought it all back to me in a rush. "He got a liver from a little boy in Indiana. That little boy is an angel."

Could it be that this woman was telling me that her son had gotten one of Bobby's organs and was now a healthy boy again because of it?

I was afraid to ask more questions because I didn't want to break the spell I was under if I was wrong. I wanted to feel like I was in God's hands somehow even if He had decided that my baby should die and hers should live. No, that wasn't it! God had decided that my baby would die *in order that* her baby might live! Where had such a choice been made before? One Son dying to save another?

That made my baby . . . somebody's savior. And it wasn't just her baby who had gotten something from Bobby. Some other people had gotten other organs from Bobby. That meant part of my child still lived and was helping some children to bring joy to their mothers.

There are more than 10,000 people who attend that church. There wasn't a doubt in my mind that Maracita and I had to meet there so that she would tell me about her Jamie.

It's possible that I'm wrong, that it was just a coincidence that her boy got a liver from a boy in Indiana, a boy whose parents were African-American and Hispanic like her boy. I'll never know for sure because hospital records are sealed. They don't tell you who got what piece of your child.

But I wasn't wrong about what I felt there in God's church with Maracita. I could have felt angry that her child lived and mine didn't. I could have felt jealous. I could have felt all those awful bad things. But I didn't. It took me a while to realize what I did feel.

Then I got it: I felt comforted. It was as if I'd been given a sign. Maracita didn't impress me as being the smartest woman in the world. But she had one thing that few people ever get. She had perfect faith that she had been blessed.

She gave me back my faith, too. Because in my heart, I knew that Bobby had been part of her blessing. Maybe I'll meet someone else one day and have another child. I hope so. There's love in me again for another baby. There's hope in me again for a better life.

Maracita said the baby who gave her boy a liver was an angel. She's right. He was when he was alive and he is now.

That much I've known all along. ✳

*I love to travel. It runs in the family.* The only thing that makes it hard to travel is that I have a lot of allergies. Despite them or maybe really because of them, my parents have always tried to take me with them on their travels. They don't want me to be hampered by my allergies. My parents have an adventurous spirit and they want me to have one, too. So, I carry a lot of medicines and I try to be careful about strange cuisines since some foods can trigger an allergic reaction. That is the only part of travel that I hate because I like to try new things. Still, watching what I eat is a small price to pay for the opportunity to explore a lot of interesting places.

Like everyone else, though, after September 11, our family was hesitant to get back in the air. But we had made plans to go to France over winter vacation and we all agreed that we should go, despite our fear. My dad said that if we gave in to the fear of flying, it would be like letting the terrorists win. My dad was more angry than scared by the terrorist attacks.

It was really a great trip! We backpacked around France and did a lot of sightseeing and shopping.

I wasn't worried about terrorism until the morning we were supposed to come home. I don't know why, but I woke up with a strange feeling of dread. I couldn't say anything about it to my parents. My mother would certainly be worried about getting on the plane—she's not superstitious but she does pay attention to what she calls people's "sixth sense." If I told her how I was feeling, she might freak out. My dad, on the other hand, would sort of laugh at me. He wouldn't make fun of me, but he'd just tell me there was no reason to feel nervous. I decided to just try and shrug it off.

I tried. I kept up conversation throughout the day and even when we got to the airport. But then that feeling got stronger. As we boarded the plane, I almost blurted out, "No! Let's take a different flight!" But I kept my mouth shut.

When my dad talked about the terrorist attacks, he talked about fear. He said there are many different kinds. There is a rational fear that is kind of like your personal safety net. It keeps you from doing harebrained things that are really dangerous. He also said there is an irrational fear that can cripple you, preventing you from accomplishing things that you want to do. This was the kind of fear he said we had to fight if we were going to continue to live our lives after September 11. I wasn't sure which category the feeling I had as I boarded that plane fell into.

The plane was only half full. I wasn't surprised because my dad had told me that many people were afraid to fly after September 11. His feeling was that with security at the airports at an all-time high, travel was safer now than ever. I believed him. In any case, my parents and I got a whole row to ourselves. I decided to stretch out and take a nap. I noticed an elderly man in the row across from me. He smiled at me and nodded. As we both helped ourselves to the blankets and pillows in the overhead bins, he said, "Looks like we both have the same idea, young lady!"

Takeoff was smooth and as we climbed, I looked out at the beautiful terrain below me. I watched it get smaller and smaller until we were so high in the clouds that all I could see was whiteness around me. I pulled down the shades, put my earphones on, and closed my eyes. I must have dozed off because we were more than an hour into the flight when I was suddenly jolted awake!

I couldn't understand what had awakened me. The plane hadn't lurched or anything. There was no sudden noise. In fact, the lights had been turned off so people could sleep through the different time zones. I did see that the flight attendants had left snacks on the trays. Mine was on the tray in the center seat, untouched. Flight attendants will just leave you alone if you are sleeping.

So what was it that woke me? I looked around. The man across the aisle was sleeping. I took another look. Something about the man looked odd to me. I don't know what made me do it because I am basically pretty shy and restrained, but I stood up in my seat and leaned over to get a better look at the man. I pulled his blanket down a little. His face was bluish and I knew immediately that he wasn't breathing.

I screamed for help! Immediately, flight attendants rushed down the aisle; other passengers stood to get a better look! What was going through the minds of the other passengers, I can only imagine.

There wasn't one doctor on that plane. Probably because there were so few people in general. But, the flight attendants knew what to do. They had some equipment and they began to work on the man. The pilot's voice came over the loud speaker, telling everyone to remain calm, that we weren't under attack. We had a medical emergency and we would be making an emergency landing as quickly as possible.

With all the adults on the plane taking charge, I don't know what made me think that I should say anything. But just then, I noticed the man's opened snack on the tray in front of him. The snack was peanuts.

Anyone with allergies knows that peanuts are potent allergens. They laid him out on the floor and then I really got a look at him.

It was his hands. They were big and red and blotchy! I screamed it so loudly, they heard me in the back of the plane over the roar of the engines! "He's allergic to peanuts!" I never travel without my epi-pen. I handed it over to the flight attendant. He took it and jabbed it into the man's thigh. Then, another worker took a vial of something out of the medical kit and gave him another shot.

Within seconds, the man's face lost its awful color and became less bloated. He coughed violently for a minute. He was sitting up, leaning against one of the flight crew as the pilot announced our landing.

We didn't get off the plane; the paramedics came on the plane with a stretcher. But the man waved them away, saying,

"I can walk!" He spoke a few words to the flight crew, probably thanking them. Then he turned to me.

"They told me it was you who discovered me. You were the one who knew what to do for me. You are a remarkable young lady." He took my hand in both of his. "My son was supposed to take this trip with me but he was afraid to fly. He is a doctor and I know he would have known what to do for me, too. You're not a doctor, but you did just as good a job as any one of them could have! Thank you for my life."

They made him sit in a wheelchair as he stepped into the hallway leading into the terminal.

It was over so quickly. My mother put her arms around me and I realized I was shaking all over. My dad told me how proud he was for my quick thinking!

I was pretty proud of myself, too. It's an amazing feeling to know that you have saved a life. Maybe I'll be a doctor someday and save a lot of lives.

I had been part of a miracle! It was all about overcoming fear. That man's son had been afraid to fly. My parents didn't want me to be afraid—not just of flying, but of living, really. They never wanted me to allow my physical problems to interfere with anything I wanted to do. And our whole family didn't want to give in to the fear of terrorism in any form.

So we had taken this trip. And I was in the right place at the right time to save a life. The whole thing just proves what my father has been saying all along. If you can just overcome your fears, anyone can accomplish anything. Even a miracle. ✳

*I* don't know how old I was when I first realized that my father had "spells." At least that was what my mother called them. Sometimes she tried to pretend that nothing was wrong, that every husband in the world came home from work, snarled a greeting at his wife and kids, and then headed straight for the liquor cabinet.

When I was little, my dad used to come home from work in a good mood. I would run to greet him at the door and he would swing me up onto his shoulders and then pretend that he couldn't find me, walking all through the house calling me, asking my mom where I could possibly be. Then he would pause in front of the hall mirror and act very surprised to see me there, sitting on his shoulders! How I loved the look on his face when he finally "found" me! I loved him so much then.

But as I got older, my father drank more. My mother told me that he was under a lot of pressure at work, that he needed some way to relax.

It got worse each year. At first, he drank only if they had friends over, and then it was only a beer or two. But then he started drinking alone—first only in the evenings, then on the weekends in the middle of the day.

Milestones in my life were defined by whether or not my

dad was drunk for the occasion. I'd look at pictures of my birthday parties and remember, "Oh, that was the party where we all went to ride the ponies. Dad only had one beer there . . ." Or "Here I am at my dance recital when I was nine. I remember the tutu and the lights. And, oh yeah, I remember how my friend Nancy whispered about my dad's breath when he leaned over to wish us good luck before our dance."

But the worst was my sixteenth birthday. That morning, my mom took me down to get my driver's license. I was so nervous but I passed on the first try! My mother was afraid to let us drive anywhere with my father, so she was relieved. When I came home with that little laminated card in my hand, I couldn't wait to show my dad. He made me take him for a drive—right to the liquor store! I was so angry as I waited outside for him that I almost left him there and drove home alone.

Finally my father's drinking caused him to lose his job. That meant he had more time around the house—more time to drink. He became very mean when he drank.

My mother took my sister and me to live in a small rented house across town. She didn't want a divorce. She still loved him.

We all prayed that he would get help. And he tried. He went to Alcoholics Anonymous and promised to change. He wanted us to be a family again. We all wanted to believe him.

He seemed better. He started coming over to the house without smelling of liquor. He looked healthier, too.

When he was drinking, my father never showed any interest in my life. But as he became sober more, he began asking me questions. I wanted to tell him all about myself—to be the little girl "found" again. I started to trust him again.

He was looking for a new job but he didn't get any offers.

One day after school, I came home to find a note from my mom telling me that she had to work late. She told me to take out some frozen dinners for my sister and myself. But I had just gotten the results of the hardest biology exam I had ever taken in my life and I had gotten the highest mark in my class. I wanted to share that with someone. Since my mom wasn't home, I decided to call my dad and tell him. Maybe he would take my sister and me out to dinner to celebrate.

There was no answer when I called. I decided to take dinner over to eat it at his place. I quickly took three frozen TV dinners and loaded them and my sister into the car. When we got to his house, I used my key to go in. I intended to cook the dinners in his oven and surprise him.

I was the one who got the surprise.

My father was passed out on the living room sofa, an empty scotch bottle next to him. I ran to the kitchen and got a glass of water and threw it in his face. He roused enough to hear me scream at him, "I hate you! You're the worst father in the world! I should have known better than to think you would ever really change! I never want to see you again!"

I don't know how I drove home, I was crying so hard. How dare he do this to us? How dare he give us hope that we could be a family again and then go and get stinking drunk?

The phone was ringing when I opened the front door. My sister answered it and I flung myself down on the couch. "It's Dad," she said.

"Tell him I said to drop dead!" My sister clapped her hand quickly over the mouthpiece. But when she said, "Dad?" into the phone again, I could tell from her expression that my father had heard me.

There are some moments in time and some words that we wish we could take back. As angry as I was when I said it, I knew that I didn't really mean it. My words hung in the air for a moment like so much dirty laundry. I felt a chill and I sat up suddenly.

I sat perfectly still on the couch for a minute. I couldn't put my finger on what had come over me. It was an odd feeling— I felt horribly guilty that I had uttered those terrible words. But I didn't really mean it. My dad would know that it was just my anger talking.

I walked into my room, undressed, and crawled into bed.

Nighttime is the time for demons—the ones that live inside your head; the ones you make for yourself. I had spent so much of my life being angry at my dad, feeling disappointed and embarrassed. Then when things had seemed to be improving, I had dared to hope . . . and he had ruined it all. I should be furious at him again. I should be resolving never to let him get close to me, never to trust him again.

But that wasn't what I was feeling. All I felt was guilt. Those terrible words had actually come out of my mouth. *Tell him I said to drop dead!*

I don't know how long I had been asleep when I heard the phone ring. Then I heard my mother's long, low wail—she sounded as if she were in pain.

I sat bolt upright! Oh, God! Had it happened? Was he dead because I said those awful words?

"Your father is at the hospital," my mother said. She kept her voice calm. "There's been an accident. I don't know how bad it is. They wouldn't say. But the nurse said he was asking for you. I'll call our neighbor to stay with your sister."

I told my mother everything in the car—how my sister and I had found him passed out, how I had screamed terrible words at him, and then how I told him to drop dead. I knew it would be my fault if anything happened to him.

My mother tried to reassure me, saying that my dad was an adult and responsible for what happened.

My brain knew that my mother was right. But my heart screamed, in pain.

He wasn't dead but he did have some head injuries. Before they took him up to surgery, I said, "Dad, I didn't mean it." He didn't answer.

Like everybody else in that waiting room, I prayed for a miracle. I asked God to let my dad live. And then I prayed for the biggest miracle I could think of—I asked God to make my dad stop drinking, to start being like he was when I was a little girl.

The surgery lasted until the sun came up. When the doctor came out to say, "He's going to be all right," he had an odd expression on his face.

"The CT scan we did when your husband was brought in showed an abnormality in one of the blood vessels in his brain. We repaired the damage and he should be fine. It was actually a blessing that he had the accident when he did. We might never have found the problem until it was too late. But I must tell you that the damage was in the part of the brain that controls memory. It is possible that he won't remember things that happened last week or even things that happened last year."

Could it be true? I wondered. Could it be that my father would have no memory of my having said such horrible things to him? Was I being given a second chance?

It turned out that we were both being given a second chance. Not only did he not remember the events of that day, but he did not remember the urge he had to drink. It was gone—completely!

I have my father—and my life—back again. ✳

*W*hen my high school guidance counselor suggested that I work with a first-grader named Yvette who lived in Chicago, I assumed Yvette had physical disabilities. I've done a lot of volunteer work during high school with children who have various physical disabilities.

Yvette was disabled, too, my counselor said. Only her disability wasn't physical. And as I thought about it, I realized that Yvette's type of disability was much worse: She couldn't read.

I tried to imagine what it would be like not to be able to read. I couldn't—not really. It was such an overwhelming concept! People who can't read are missing out on so much! Not everyone can travel and explore new cultures and places. But if you can read, you can go anywhere in your own imagination! Not being able to read would be stifling, unbearable, I thought.

But I didn't know how to begin to teach her. I had absolutely no experience with teaching this kind of child. My counselor knew this. Why had he selected me to teach this little girl? I was afraid for her and for myself if I failed.

When I first met Yvette, she was timid. She seemed afraid to ask for help, afraid of me. It unnerved me. I couldn't understand and Yvette couldn't articulate her fears. Perhaps she found it overwhelming to have someone pay so much attention just to her. She came from a big family. I knew that often when she got home from school, her mother wasn't there.

I asked Yvette about herself. Little by little, she told me things. She liked animals, especially kittens and bunnies. Her neighbor down the hall had one of each and let her hold them. She had a favorite doll that an aunt had given her for her birthday. Her sister had made a dress for the doll out of some material that she had bought. She didn't like her older brother because he was always picking on her. Her older sister did her hair for her.

I began to understand what life was like for her. She didn't have very much. People didn't give her much either in the way of material things or in the way of intangibles like praise and concern. Mostly what she'd gotten from the adults in her life was the feeling that she wasn't very bright and she wasn't worth the trouble it would take to teach her to read. I wasn't an adult, but I could try to teach her to read. And if I succeeded, she'd have something of her own—something she needed desperately—a feeling of self-worth. She'd also have an avenue to escape her world and explore some aspects of life that she'd never known before.

I brought Yvette a book about kittens. The words were written in large type and accompanied by pictures. Yvette loved it. She quickly learned the sound of the letters in the words that went with the pictures—k and t and n as in "kitten." Then we tried to put together other words with the same letters and she sounded them out. "Kick" and "nut" and "kite" came next.

When we first began, Yvette brought me her report card. Her teacher had written that Yvette was behind the class and did not seem able to learn. I think Yvette believed that what the teacher said was true. Her mother and brother and sister believed that teacher and they had never even tried to teach Yvette to read. That made me angry. When a person in authority tells a child that he or she is dumb or smart, the child believes him or her. Children will rise—or sink—to the level of expectation that others have for them. No one expected anything from Yvette and that was what she was prepared to give.

When we finished the first book, I went back to the library and got another. And another, all about things that interested Yvette. One was about dolls. Another was about a little girl who wore her hair in braids like Yvette did. And with each book, Yvette learned more and more sounds. One day, she made it haltingly through several sentences. I didn't interrupt her or prompt her. It took a long time—almost the whole half hour we were together. But she did it herself. Then, she looked up at me; her eyes spoke volumes.

There was something beautiful and moving about Yvette's eyes. I had trouble understanding it until she began to sound out the letters. Then I realized that I could see a sadness in them. They had no light. It made me want to cry.

We worked with flash cards and I read stories to her out of books that were too hard for her to read herself but not too hard for her to understand and enjoy. One day, Yvette brought me a homework assignment that she had turned in. At the top, the teacher—the one who had said this child couldn't learn—had drawn a smiley face. It couldn't match the one on Yvette's face or on mine, but both of us were glad to see it.

And oh! The light in those eyes!

I was beginning to feel very good about myself. I really thought that I had done a terrific thing, teaching a child to read. Then I finally met Yvette's mother at the school when she came to pick up her daughter.

"I know you don't think I care about my baby but I do," she said. She was young, much younger than I imagined. She had beautiful brown silky skin and her eyes were Yvette's eyes. "I need to work just to feed them," she told me. "There are only the four of us since Yvette's daddy left. It's all I can do to keep the older two in school. The teacher told me that Yvette couldn't learn. I didn't believe her but I just figured I couldn't do anything about it. Then I realized I could do something. I could pray. So I did. Hard. And look at this! Here you are."

I told her that teaching Yvette to read had only taken caring and patience and persistence.

She looked at me strangely. Then she said, "Child, you listen to me. There were twelve other little girls in Yvette's grade that needed help. The teacher had a list, only she never even put Yvette on it because she didn't think anyone could help her. When I found out about the list, I was going to come in and beg that teacher to put Yvette on the list. But before I could get here, Yvette came home and told me she had a teacher, a *real* teacher. You."

We both stood there for a minute looking at each other. It took a minute for Yvette's mom's words to sink in. Then a strange feeling came over me. It was as if this woman and I were the only two people in the world at that moment. I looked into her eyes and realized with a shock that I recognized the same glow of pride in them as in Yvette's eyes.

I remembered how I had come to be Yvette's tutor. I hadn't understood why my counselor had chosen me. Now, I began to think he hadn't chosen me. Someone more powerful had. Someone who had a plan for getting Yvette and me together.

Her mother believed it was a miracle and in that moment, I did, too. And I kept on believing it each Wednesday throughout that year when I looked into the smiling happy eyes of a little dark-haired girl who knows she can accomplish anything. And I'll continue to believe it each morning when I look into the mirror and see what Yvette's mom saw that day at the school, what she had prayed for to help her little girl— a real teacher. ✳

*It wasn't a big thing really, just lifting* a few drinks, some candy maybe, sometimes a CD or two. We all did it. But I got caught. I'm not a bad kid and I don't get into trouble. I just did it for kicks. But getting caught was bad, real bad. I knew my parents would lose it. They don't live together, so when I got arrested and the cops asked me whom they should call, I thought it over. I decided my father would be less likely to overreact. He didn't react at all. He refused to come down to bail me out, so I spent the night in jail.

It was the worst night of my life and I was so scared, I couldn't close my eyes or even cry. I couldn't wait for daylight.

The next morning when that cell door opened and I saw my mom standing out in the station room, I was so happy to see her! She burst into tears.

I had a public defender. The judged sentenced me to 500 hours of community service and virtual house arrest when I wasn't working or going to school. The penalty for violating the house arrest, he warned, would be jail time.

Community service meant working in a nursing home both days of the weekend every weekend until the 500 hours had been used up. I couldn't think of anything more disgusting than going to that nursing home full of old, dirty, smelly people. I had to mop the floors using some kind of disinfectant that is supposed to mask the smells but of course doesn't do anything. I had to clean bathrooms and empty garbage and anything else one of the supervisors or nurses decided to tell me to do. They weren't making any attempt to be nice to a "felon." More than once, one of the supervisors warned me that my time could be extended if I did a bad job or bothered any of the residents. So I resolved to just show up, do what I had to do, mind my business, and get it over with.

Very few of the residents in the home ever had relatives come to visit. Most of them probably didn't know it; they were pretty out of it. But some of them had pictures in their rooms. Children and grandchildren, cards and notes were tacked on some of the residents' bulletin boards. But I never saw any visitors even in those rooms.

On my third Saturday there, I was assigned to clean the floor in a different wing. I noticed a guy in a wheelchair watching me. I was surprised by his appearance. He was much younger than the other inhabitants of the home, by about twenty years. His hair was long and he wore it pulled back in a ponytail. He wore shorts and had had one leg amputated just above the knee. I wondered about him, about the leg, about why he was in a nursing home if he wasn't old. But I was afraid to ask him anything. I didn't want to get in trouble and risk extending my sentence. But he approached me.

"How would you like me to get you a different job assignment?" he asked.

"Sure," I answered. Anything was better than what I was doing.

"I need someone to entertain me, to keep me out of trouble. What do you think?"

He didn't look like he was capable of getting into too much trouble, but I didn't want to insult him, so I just said, "Yeah, sure."

The next week, the supervisor stopped me at the supply closet as I was about to pick up my mop and bucket. He said, "Clem wants you to take him outside today. He needs some fresh air."

Clem was my ponytailed, wheelchair-bound new best friend. He was waiting for me when I knocked on his door. I thanked him for springing me from my disgusting other work details. "Ready to roll?" I asked, then winced at my own pun.

He grinned. I walked around behind him to push the wheelchair but he said sharply, "Don't do that! I can get myself to the damn door. Just open it for me, will ya? Why they make 'em so heavy for us gimps I'll never know." I pushed open the heavy metal door that led to the enclosed park in the back of the home.

"Let's park it under that big old oak," Clem said. "Did you bring anything to eat? No? Well, next time bring candy— lots of it!"

This was going to be better than I thought! Clem was an interesting guy and he liked to talk to me. Not about anything in particular. But he seemed to know a lot of stuff. He liked music (not my taste) and reading. He read anything he could get his hands on—magazines, newspapers, and books. And he liked to talk about what he knew. I found if I just asked a single question or made some casual remark, Clem would take off from there. If I mentioned a baseball team, he would tell me about some spectacular game he saw where there were five home runs or the pitcher pitched a no-hitter. He knew every statistic on every player on every team in both leagues!

He asked me why I was doing community service and I told him. I told him about my night in jail. I was about to tell him how my parents reacted when he surprised me by saying, "Don't tell me, let me guess. Your old man let you sit it out all night and your mamma cried when she had to bail you out the next day, right?"

"How did you know?" I asked, surprised. But Clem just grinned.

He lectured me on stealing, on my choice of friends, and on my treatment of my parents. But he also listened to me, too. I told him about my parents' split and how my dad didn't come to cue me very often. I also told him that the guys I had hung around with thought it was a joke to shoplift. When I got caught, though, they dropped me flat. Clem laughed at that. "Best thing that ever happened to you!"

The things he did not talk about were how he came to be in the nursing home, how he lost his leg and ended up in the wheelchair. I started to ask him once but he let me know right away that he wasn't interested in telling me.

I brought him candy and gum. He liked chocolate and hard candies. He usually ate just one piece and then hid the rest to save for during the week.

One Monday morning, I woke up for school as usual. But I felt awful. My stomach hurt and the room was spinning. I wanted to stay home but I couldn't without permission. I called my mother and told her I was sick and asked her to please call the school to tell them. It's a stupid rule but since I got arrested, I have to do everything by the book.

My mother sounded unhappy but agreed. She told me she would check on me later.

I turned on the TV. Daytime TV is enough to make you sick if you aren't already. I tried to find something that wasn't a soap opera. We don't have cable.

I turned to some medical news show. What caught my attention was a diabetes patient in a wheelchair! Sick as I felt, I sat up and looked hard at the image on the screen. It wasn't Clem but it could have been.

The patient in the wheelchair was a man in his fifties with long hair pulled back in a ponytail. His right leg had had to be amputated just below the knee because of complications from his disease. He was learning to walk using a prosthesis—a fake leg.

He looked so much like Clem! Was Clem also a diabetic? Is that how he lost his leg? Diabetics can't have sugar and I had been bringing him candy . . . was I hurting him? Or helping him hurt himself? I was so sick, my mind must have been playing tricks. I was suddenly scared that something bad was happening to Clem! Right that very minute!

I wasn't supposed to leave the apartment without permission and besides I felt horrible. I called the nursing home and asked to speak to the floor nurse on Clem's floor. But she was busy and they put me on hold. I hung up and called back. The line was busy. I tried again. And again.

I knew I had to get there no matter how awful I felt.

They knew my schedule at the home, so when I burst through the front door, the secretary looked startled to see me. It was all I could do to get the words out of my mouth.

"Clem, the guy with the ponytail. I've been bringing him candy. He's my friend. He asked me to. I don't know if he's diabetic or something. Can you check on him? Is he okay?" The words came out in a rush. Then I passed out.

What happened while I was out cold was related to me by about twenty staff members who were huddled around me when I came to about an hour later.

Someone had gone to check on Clem because I had seemed so sure that he was in trouble. He was, though not for the reason I thought. He wasn't a diabetic. That wasn't why he asked me to bring him candy.

Instead, Clem was giving his candy away to the elderly residents he spent time with—residents who never had any other visitors!

Then the supervisor told me how they had found Clem. "He was in another wing visiting a patient—an old man. The man wasn't breathing! He was choking on a piece of candy that Clem had given him! When Clem tried to help him—he must have tried to get out of his wheelchair—he fell and hit his head. He was just out of reach of the nurse's call button when we found the two of them! Luckily, we were able to give the old man in the bed the Heimlich maneuver and the candy popped out! He's going to be fine! So is Clem! But it was a miracle that we found them when we did. Another few minutes and that old man would be dead! And poor Clem . . . well, he wouldn't want that on his conscience. Good thing you came!

"I have just one question—what made you think Clem was a diabetic?" the supervisor asked me. I told him what I had seen on TV.

The supervisor said, "Clem lost his leg in a car accident. Don't ask him for details though. He doesn't like to talk about it. He was driving and his family was killed."

"Why doesn't Clem just get a fake leg?" I asked. "Then he could walk and live on his own."

I saw the nurse and my supervisor exchange glances before my supervisor said, "I think Clem doesn't feel that he deserves to have a leg. He likes living here, thinks he has a purpose. Maybe he does. You should see how much better the folks do who get a visit and some candy from Clem. When he misses a day, those old people are just miserable."

I thought about that for a minute. "Kind of like a community service sentence he put on himself, isn't it?" I said.

Then I realized that a life was saved that day because of

me! And if I hadn't gotten there when I did and made the staff look for Clem, the old man in the bed would have choked to death. And Clem would have felt responsible!

Suddenly, I realized that I didn't feel sick anymore. In fact, I never felt better! Well, of course, I had to feel sick to stay home to watch that program. If I hadn't seen it, I never would have been thinking of Clem and I wouldn't have arrived at the home when I did. It all made perfect sense. But it was very complicated. No human being could have made it all happen that way.

No human being did, I was sure.

My community service ended that summer, but not my visits to see Clem. Only now I bring lollipops. ✳

*I* got Odie on my twelfth birthday. He was just a pup. We named him Odysseus because right from the start, he made it clear that he liked to get out of the yard and roam the neighborhood. (Odysseus was an explorer, a character in a book I had to read in school.) Odysseus was a silly name for such a funny-looking little puppy, so I just called him Odie. He's a great dog and he loves everybody. Sometimes he loves people a little too much as I found out one afternoon when I let him out as I usually did when I came home from school.

Somehow I forgot to make sure the gate was closed tightly and Odie got out of the yard. I didn't realize it until I went to call him in about a half hour later. He was gone!

At first I didn't worry. Odie had tags on. The animal warden had picked Odie up once before, and we had to pay a fine. I knew that this time, I'd be the one to pay it.

But when we called the animal warden to report our dog missing, the warden said no one had turned him in. The next day, when Odie still hadn't been found, I really started to panic! I'm sixteen but I felt like crying. That dog is really special. I've had him for four years and I can't even remember what life was like without him.

Odie was gone for two days. On Saturday night, the door-bell rang. I was home doing nothing since I didn't feel much like being with my friends. When I answered the door, I was surprised to see a stranger on our doorstep.

She had an accent. "I found your little dog. Don't worry, he is fine. He is keeping my sister Clara company, but I will return him right away if you want. But I am hoping that you will let him stay with us for a little while."

I called my mother to the door. To my surprise, she invited the lady in and asked her to sit down.

Her name was Greta Slepak. Odie's dog tag had our phone number and she had used the reverse directory to come in person.

I was beginning to get really nervous. Why didn't she just return my dog? Did she want money or something? I was starting to imagine all sorts of terrible things but I kept my mouth shut.

"My sister Clara is very sick," Mrs. Slepak explained. "She has a form of cancer for which there is no cure. And it is painful. The pain has kept her from doing any of the things she loves. She loves to visit with people and to cook. She loves dogs. She wanted me to go to the animal shelter and get one for her but I just couldn't bring myself to do it. I love dogs too, but if I bought one just for Clara and then she died . . . well, I couldn't keep it and it wouldn't be fair to the animal. But the other day Clara was sitting outside in the yard and along came your dog! How he made her smile!

"Clara will be sixty next month. We are planning a big birthday party for her. All of Clara's children and grandchildren will come. They live in other cities but everyone has promised to come for the party."

Mrs. Slepak stopped speaking and I saw my mother reach for her hand. Women do things like that. Both of them had tears in their eyes. Then I got it! The party would be Clara's last visit with everybody. She was close to death.

But what did this have to do with Odie?

Mrs. Slepak explained. "My sister has pancreatic cancer. The doctor told her three weeks ago and from that moment, she became an invalid. It was as if she had given up all hope! But when she saw your dog—what a change! Clara got up out of the chair and went inside to cook dinner. Clara loves to cook, really cook—full-course dinners! She invited friends and there were ten of us at the table! Ten—and your dog! He loved Clara's dinner, too."

Well at least I knew Odie had been well treated. I started to say something but my mother shushed me.

"Will your sister have treatment?" my mother wanted to know.

"Well, that's just it. Originally she said no, because chemotherapy is bad. She didn't want to go through it all—the nausea and losing her hair. But this morning when she got up, she said that she is willing to try. She wants to be at her party next month."

Mrs. Slepak looked at me then. "Your dog has given my

sister some hope. I know you love your dog, but could we please just borrow him for a little while? He is such a comfort to my sister. Maybe he can bring some joy to her, for however long she has left?"

Before I could even open my mouth, I heard my mother say, "Of course, Odie can stay for a few weeks. Steven will come and walk him for you."

Mrs. Slepak gave her address and left. She seemed nice and I felt bad about her sister. I would still get to see Odie because I was going to have to go over there every day to walk him, so I guessed I didn't mind lending out my dog.

The next day after school, I went over. They lived about three miles away. It amazed me that Odie had gotten so far that day in so little time, especially since he likes to take his time on a walk and sniff everything that isn't moving. And he had to have crossed two busy streets. It really was a miracle he wasn't killed.

It was a miracle he found Mrs. Slepak's house at all. It's tucked away down a dead-end street. If I hadn't been told how to get there, I wouldn't have found it.

Odie bounded to the door and wagged his tail like usual when I walked in. He jumped all over me. He was happy to see me. He probably would want to go home after our walk, I thought.

To my complete and utter shock, though, as soon as Mrs. Slepak opened the door, Odie leaped inside and ran over to Clara, who was sitting on the couch.

Odie planted himself at Clara's feet and looked up at me. His tail thumped wildly.

Clara said, "Thank you. He's wonderful, isn't he? Will you come tomorrow?" I was a little disappointed that Odie wanted to stay, but I just told Clara yes, I would come every day.

As I stood to go, I expected Odie to follow me. But Odie just sat there, next to Clara, wagging his tail.

Odie stayed with Mrs. Slepak and her sister for five weeks. I went every day to visit, to play with my dog, and to walk him. I wanted him to remember me and want to come home again. I often ate dinner at the Slepaks'. Clara was a great cook even though she made food with names I couldn't pronounce. She told me about her three children.

I liked the sisters. They were smart and funny—and really close to one another. I felt sorry that Clara was so sick. I knew that she was going for chemotherapy because her hair fell out. But she wore these huge, brightly colored bandannas. She seemed to have a lot of energy.

Everyone was coming for the big party and Clara was doing all the cooking for it. She made me taste everything. Odie did, too, and he loved her food. I wondered how I would ever get him back to eating dog food.

The party was on a Saturday night. For two days before, I helped them set up chairs, made runs to the airport to pick up their relatives, and took care of Odie. Odie was invited to the party but I wasn't. I didn't mind. I understood it was a family thing and even though that sort of meant they considered Odie a part of their family, I wasn't upset. He made Clara so happy!

On the Sunday morning after the party, I got a phone call. "Odie is ready to come home now," Mrs. Slepak's voice said. "Could you please come get him, though? I can't leave right now." Something in her voice made me pause for a minute. "Is everything all right?" I asked.

I knew the answer before she even opened her mouth to reply.

"Clara went into the hospital early this morning. She's in a coma. The cancer is everywhere and it won't be much longer." Mrs. Slepak wasn't crying but I was.

Clara died quietly later that day and Odie was contentedly licking himself in our backyard just as if he had never left.

Mrs. Slepak thanked us a lot for letting Odie stay with her until Clara's death. Odie's presence in Clara's life had been a real miracle, enabling her to have some joy in her final days. Mrs. Slepak said she didn't know how Odie had found them or why he wanted to stay with Clara, but she was glad he had.

D-o-g spelled backward is g-o-d. I know how Odie had gotten there and I knew why he stayed. He was listening to a different Master.

When I was fifteen, I thought I knew everything. Well, the important things, anyway. I certainly didn't know everything about algebra or U.S. history. But I knew how to take care of myself, and that my parents were way too protective. So I figured that what they didn't know couldn't hurt them.

I was wrong, however. I found out that what they didn't know not only could hurt them, but it could hurt me, too.

I liked to think I was pretty. But, like most teenage girls, I had some doubts. I spent hours in front of the mirror trying on outfits and doing my hair before school every morning. I surreptitiously checked out my reflection in the store windows when I walked down the street with my friends. But the most important reflection wasn't made of glass. It was the boys.

To my friends and me, making an impression on a boy was the ultimate goal. If a boy turned and looked when you walked down the hall at school, it was the highlight of the day. For a while, the boys just looked, and that was enough for us. But it seemed that after a while, we needed more. To get a boy in the school, even a senior, to look at you was one thing. But we needed constant reassurance, and we needed to know where the limits were. Did we really look like those girls on the cover of *Seventeen*? Just how pretty and sophisticated were we?

The way to test this, of course, was to hang around older guys. But this wasn't so easy to do. Most of them were away at college, and the ones who weren't, the ones who worked at the gas station or the tire factory, we considered to be losers.

One night, however, we discovered that there was an easy way to attract the guys. In fact, it was right under our noses. It happened on a Saturday night, when my friend Diane and I had gone to see a movie. Her mother was supposed to pick us up at 10:15, but the movie ended earlier than we had thought. We were going to call her, but it was a beautiful summer night, and we wanted to stay out a little bit longer. There wasn't really much to do, however. It was a small town. There was one main street, which had the movie theater, the post office, and an assortment of shops and restaurants. We decided to get Cokes at the pizza place next door, and then wait in the park across the street.

As we waited to cross the street, a car slowed down. The driver honked the horn and a boy leaned his head out of the window and whistled. Then the car sped away.

I was thrilled and terrified at the same time. It was exciting and flattering to have boys notice us. But I wasn't quite sure I really wanted the attention.

Diane was sure, though. She wanted more of it, and she convinced me to go along. I was always following her, it seemed. She was so self-confident, I thought, so brave. And she was beautiful. I envied her thick, shiny hair and her perfect figure. And besides, she was really nice. I liked being with her.

So this quickly became our regular Saturday night activity: We would tell our parents that we were going to someone's house or to the 7-Eleven to get ice cream. Then we would head off for downtown. The walk was about two miles, but we didn't mind.

When we got there, we would walk down the main street of town. We always made sure to wear our shortest skirts or our tightest pants. It never took long for the cars to start slowing, the horns to start honking. We considered it a game. We counted how many cars would honk in fifteen minutes. I was still a little nervous, but it seemed safe enough.

Then, one night, a car slowed as it passed us. Then it stopped. A guy poked his head out of the window and called out to us. I stopped where I was, but Diane pulled my arm. "Come on," she said. "I'm just going to talk to them."

"I don't know . . . ," I began.

"Come on! Don't be a baby!" she insisted. I followed her reluctantly.

The car waited at the curb. It was dark, but as we got closer, I could see that there were three boys in the car. Older boys. Maybe old enough to be in college, I guessed. The one riding in the front seat opened the door and swung his legs out onto the curb. "Hi," he said.

"Hi, yourself," Diane answered brightly. I didn't say anything. He asked us our names. He told us he was from New York, and that he was here visiting his cousin. After a few minutes, he threw his cigarette into the gutter. "You want to go for a ride?" he asked.

"No thanks," I started to say. But I was shocked to realize

that Diane was saying yes. What was she thinking? "No, let's just go home," I urged her.

"Come on, it'll be fun," she said. She turned back to the boy. "Just for a few minutes, okay?" she said.

"Sure, whatever you want," he answered. "Just for a few minutes."

Diane turned back to me. "Come on," she said quietly. "I don't want to go alone. And I don't want to leave you here alone, either."

The oddest feeling came over me. I had an overwhelming sense that this wasn't just a carefree group of guys looking to take two cute girls for a ride. It wasn't that they looked any different from the other boys we had seen around town. It was just something . . . really evil about them. I don't know why I didn't just refuse. The words wouldn't come out of my mouth. I was used to going along with Diane, used to following her lead. Shocked, scared down to my toes, I heard myself say, "Okay."

Diane got into the car first. I couldn't think of a way out of this! I started to get in. Suddenly I heard another car honk. Only it wasn't just a tap on the horn; it was a blast like a foghorn! What car made a sound like that? I looked up. A figure got out of a small car but I couldn't immediately see who it was. The figure stood for a moment backlit in the headlights of the car. I stared for what seemed like a long time. Something was familiar about the figure; I knew it was probably someone I knew but for just that fleeting instant, whoever it was looked a little ghostly in the headlights.

Then, she said my name!

I froze where I was standing. The person called my name again, and then she was standing next to me. It was Mrs. Marshall, a friend of my mother's. I was stunned for just a minute and my mouth must have dropped open. Then I shut it with a pop and shook myself slightly. Of course, it wasn't any angel (that's what I was thinking she looked like in the head-lights). Pretty stupid of me.

I swore to myself. I should have known something like this could happen, I thought. My mother knows everybody in this town. I was stupid to think no one would see me.

Mrs. Marshall looked at me, and then she looked into the car. "Hello, Diane," she said.

"Hi," Diane answered meekly.

"You look like you could use a ride home," she said.

"Thanks," I managed to answer, as Diane climbed out of the backseat.

Mrs. Marshall didn't say anything on the way home. We dropped Diane off at her house. "Call me tomorrow," Diane said to me as she got out of the car.

We drove to my house in silence. When we pulled into the driveway, Mrs. Marshall turned off the engine. I was dreading the scene I was sure would follow, when Mrs. Marshall would escort me into the house and tell my parents exactly how she happened to be driving me home.

"You know, your mother is a really good friend of mine," she said.

"I know," I answered, wondering where this was leading.

"And it's going to be really hard for me to talk to her every day and not tell her about this," she continued. "But maybe I can do it, if you'll promise me you'll never, ever do that again."

I nodded. "I promise," I said.

"You know, I assume, how stupid and dangerous that was?" she asked.

"Yes, I know," I said. "I don't even know why I did it. I didn't really want to."

"Well, that's it, then. Tell Diane that I won't tell your parents, but I'm trusting both of you to keep your end of the deal."

I was so relieved that I wanted to cry. "Thank you," I said. "Don't worry, I will never do that again. It was dumb."

"Really dumb," Mrs. Marshall agreed. "You're lucky I came by when I did. You know, I really just made a wrong turn on my way home from work. That's how I happened to be there. It's funny, really. I know this town like the back of my hand. How could I have missed my turn? I wonder . . . Well, go on inside now, it's late."

A couple of days later, I read in the local paper that a teenage girl over in the next town had been raped. The police were looking for a car with New York license plates.

After we read that newspaper, Diane and I knew that Mrs. Marshall had no control over missing her turn. She was meant to see us, to save us.

Someone was looking out for us that night—and it wasn't the boys. ✳

*My little brother Andrew is retarded.*
I know I'm supposed to say "handicapped" or "cognitively disabled." But that's like putting a mask over what I really want to
say: He's retarded. He looks weird, he acts strange, and he
talks funny. People make fun of him and he doesn't even know
it. I know I should stick up for him, but sometimes it's really
hard because he is always incredibly difficult and annoying.

This last summer was no different. We went on our annual
family camping trip in South Dakota, where we go hiking, rock
climbing, and white-water rafting.

I managed to get through the first couple of days of the trip
by ignoring Andrew as much as I could. It was hard, though.
Andrew is constantly telling everyone what to do. "The tent's
not zipped," he would say all the time. "The bugs are getting in!
Zip up the tent! Zip up the tent!" He said it every time someone
came in or out of the tent, until I couldn't stand it anymore.

"All right, Andrew!" I screamed at him. "You don't need to
keep saying it all the time!"

My mom got mad at me. She said that I need to be more
patient, that Andrew functions best when things are predictable
and follow a routine. But just knowing that doesn't make his
behavior any less annoying.

The day we went white-water rafting, Andrew was a pain from the moment he woke up. My parents wanted to give us donuts to eat in the car, instead of taking the time to eat breakfast at the campground. But Andrew refused.

"No, Mom!" he complained. "At the table! We have to eat at the table!" He kept repeating it over and over until my mother finally gave in. Sometimes, that's the only way to get him to shut up.

Finally, we got to the river. We all climbed into the raft, which was equipped with six life jackets. Each of us selected one and put it on. We left the extra one in the bottom of the raft and paddled out into the river. Andrew was fairly quiet, and he was too excited to bug anyone. After a while, we reached a calm place in the river, and we all stopped paddling and just sat back while the raft drifted slowly along. I took off my life jacket and leaned back and closed my eyes.

As soon as Andrew noticed that I'd taken off my life jacket, he was on me like a swarm of hornets.

"Amy, put on your life jacket! Amy's not wearing her life jacket, Mom! That's dangerous! Amy, put your life jacket back on!"

My parents tried to reassure him, but Andrew wouldn't let up. He kept pleading and demanding. Finally, even my mother couldn't stand it.

"Amy, just put the life jacket back on," she told me. "It's just not worth it—he's ruining the trip for all of us."

I hated giving in to him, but I knew better than to argue with my mother.

I grabbed one of the jackets and started to put it on. But instead of being satisfied, Andrew suddenly started screaming.

"No, that's the wrong one! Amy, put *your* jacket on! Put *your* jacket on!"

I wanted to kill him! What difference did it make? They were exactly the same. But I couldn't stand listening to Andrew scream, so I put down the jacket I was holding and put on the other one. Immediately Andrew calmed down. There, I thought, now maybe we can have some peace.

No sooner had the thought entered my head when the raft lurched. We had drifted into a rougher, faster part of the river. The raft was moving faster every second. I tried to grab for the rope on the side. But then, unexpectedly, the raft jerked sharply to one side. The next thing I knew, I was underwater.

Frantically, I fought my way to the surface. The water was swirling around me. I was whisked along too, helpless in the rushing water. "Help!" I tried to scream, but the water rushed into my mouth.

Then, suddenly, I was no longer moving. The strap on my life jacket had wrapped itself tightly around a thick vine protruding from the water. I heard someone screaming from the shore, telling me to hold on.

The raft, with the rest of my family in it, had disappeared downstream. But another raft, this one holding two men, was paddling toward me. I don't know how they did it, because the current felt so strong. I watched, terrified, as the raft lurched through the water toward me, and the men steered it around broadside. In one motion, one of them leaned out of the raft as it passed me. He reached over with a knife and cut the jacket strap that had anchored me, while the other man hauled me up into the raft. I could only lie on the bottom of the raft, gasping, while the raft moved swiftly downriver to a calm place. As we came ashore, I saw my parents and my brother and sister waving frantically. I started to cry.

"I was so scared," I sobbed, even though it had all happened so quickly that I hadn't really had time to think about anything. My mom hugged me tightly.

I started to take off my life jacket. The strap where the man had cut it was still long enough to dangle down a bit.

"She's lucky," the man told my parents. "You know, it was really a miracle that the jacket she was wearing had that long strap. That's what snagged on the branch. If she'd been wearing any of these other jackets . . ." His voice trailed off, and we all looked at the other life jackets that everyone was still holding. All of the jackets looked exactly the same, and none of them had a too-long strap hanging down—none of them except mine.

"Are you okay, Amy?" Andrew was saying anxiously. "Are you okay? Are you okay?" He looked scared.

"It's okay, Andrew, I'm fine. You can stop worrying," I told him.

"Amy fell out of the raft. She fell in the water. She fell in the water. She fell in," he said to the other boaters who were standing on the beach. Some of them gave him funny looks, but he just kept right on talking.

"She's okay, she put on her life jacket, it was *her* life jacket, not the other one. She put on the *right* one," he said.

"I told her to put it on," he continued. "I told her to put it on. The right one. *The right one, not the wrong one!*"

That was true, I realized. I had only put on the life jacket because Andrew insisted, because he was bugging me so much that I couldn't stand it, because he wouldn't let up until everything was right. *Exactly* right.

My jacket, that particular jacket, had saved me because it had a strap that caught on some vines and anchored me in place. It didn't just keep my head out of the water. It kept me from being swept down the river.

The other people were still looking at Andrew strangely. But this time, instead of getting mad at Andrew, I was mad at those people. If it wasn't for Andrew, I wanted to tell them, I wouldn't have put that life jacket on. If it wasn't for Andrew, bugging me and insisting that everything be *exactly* the way it was supposed to be, I would have been unable to stop in the current; I would have drowned.

I walked over to Andrew and put my arm around him.

"You're right, Andrew," I said. "You told me to put it on. You were right."

But Andrew wasn't even listening. He was following a group of boaters down to the water's edge.

"Don't forget your life jackets," he was saying. "Put on your life jackets. Put on your life jackets!"

And they all did. ✳

*My whole life, I have been legally* blind. While I had some sight, I never knew when I woke up in the morning exactly how much vision I would have that day.

I have a condition called dry-eye syndrome: My eyes do not produce enough tears to lubricate my corneas. As a result, my corneas were scarred. Glasses couldn't help me.

The only thing that really bothered me was that I couldn't drive, and I was jealous of all of my friends.

But I was never one to dwell on what I couldn't do. Instead, I concentrated on doing the things I could do. I played varsity basketball in high school. My teammates gave me oral signals and I learned to gauge where the ball was by the sound of their voices. As a result I learned to focus extremely well. I was nick-named "Blindman" and awarded the sportsmanship trophy my senior year. I also worked on the school newspaper, taking interviews on my tape recorder, and I was on student council.

I had plenty of friends and I got the chance to travel. I spent two years in Israel before I went to college. I guess I was pretty lucky because I didn't feel completely deprived by my blindness.

But I never stopped hoping for a miracle.

As a religious person, I have always prayed regularly. For

seventeen years, I asked God to restore my vision. But I got used to the idea that it would never happen. For whatever reason, God wanted me to be the way I am. It wasn't so bad.

One day my mother called me at college. That day, she had gone to take the trash out and noticed that all the news-papers had been picked up except for one section. That section was opened to an article about a man from a neighboring town who had vision problems.

For a reason she still doesn't understand, my mother picked up that dirty, lonely piece of newspaper and read the article. The story was about a Dr. Perry Rosenthal at the Boston Foundation for Sight in Massachusetts. Dr. Rosenthal had developed a special pair of contact lenses that enabled the man in the article to regain enough vision to get his driver's license.

But when my mother called our family eye doctor, he said, "Don't get Jason's hopes up. It probably won't help him. His vision is too far gone." And that was that. My mother forgot about the article. She even put it into the recycling bin again.

But the next day, when she went to take the trash out, again all the newspapers had been picked up except the page with the article about the special contact lenses on it.

All day, my mother had tried to take her mind off the article, but somehow the fact that it was still there, just outside, gnawed at her.

When she opened the mail that day, she nearly fainted. Among the usual mail was an envelope with no return address. She opened to find inside a copy of the article with a note that said, "You might be interested in this!" It was unsigned!

Mom made me an appointment before she even called me to tell me about it. It was probably a good thing she did, too, because I had been disappointed so many times, I'm not sure I would have pursued it on my own.

"Are you kidding?" my mother almost shouted at me. "It was there not once but twice after I had thrown it out! And then it appeared in the mail. Who sent it? Someone who obviously means for you to go to this doctor, to try one more time! Where is your faith? Don't you see?"

Not the best choice of words but she got her point across. I agreed to travel to Boston to see Dr. Rosenthal. My parents were to meet me there. We would have to spend two weeks in Boston trying the contact lenses and getting used to them.

The night before I left, I said my regular prayers. For once, I didn't ask God to restore my vision. I think a part of me was afraid to think, like my mother obviously did, that this time was going to be different, that this time I would get my miracle. And I also wondered what I would be like if I weren't blind. God made me the way I was. Should I hope to be different?

I now know that if my mother had thrown that article out 100 times, it still would have appeared somehow in a place where she would find it. She was meant to—just as I was meant to put those lenses in my eyes and see my own eyelashes for the first time. When God wants you to have a miracle, He doesn't give up until you finally get it. Until you finally see.

I did.

My dad's face was the first thing I saw when I looked up from the mirror after the lenses were in. "I never realized how ugly you are!" I joked. I could see every pore and wrinkle on his face—and the tears in his eyes. I'd never seen anyone more beautiful in my whole life.

My parents took me for a ride. I read every license plate and street sign we passed. I noticed that there were individual leaves on the trees and pebbles in the sidewalk. When we went home to Chicago two weeks later, I walked all around my neighborhood, reliving my childhood, really seeing things for the first time.

The neighbor's white picket fence battered by years of baseballs hit into it. Every scratch and nick was wonderful. The individual bricks that made up my house and each step leading up to the front door. Every crack in every sidewalk. It was all wonderful and beautiful and amazing.

Then I went to visit my grandparents. I cried when I saw them. It was the first time I could see I looked like my grandfather. My grandmother said, "See, Jason, if you live long enough, anything is possible."

As we drove home, I knew she was right. Anything is possible because God does grant miracles. You just have to have the vision to appreciate it. Now, I appreciate every petal, every leaf, every ant and bug and grasshopper. It's true what they say—God is in the details.

When I was a sophomore in high school, my little sister Julie died of leukemia. She was twelve years old. When she was diagnosed with the disease three years earlier, the doctors at first gave us lots of hope. The statistics were with her, they said. Children her age who fit a certain set of criteria usually have a remission, they said. I learned a lot of new words that year.

The doctors said they would consider her cured if she stayed in remission for five years. Everyone in our family fixated on that milestone. If we could only reach it, I would make her the biggest, best surprise party for her fourteenth birthday! If only . . .

Julie fought her disease with all of her strength and I tried to give her some of mine. I really believed that she would get better.

Toward the end, Julie reached a point where she just couldn't face any more treatments. They made her so sick and weak. But I wanted her to fight. I didn't want to let her go.

Julie liked me to read to her. She didn't care what it was as long as she could concentrate on the sound of my voice instead of the pain. One day when I came home from school, I could tell right away that it had been a bad day for her. She wanted me to read to her so she could fall asleep. But the only book I had brought home was my Freshman English Lit book. We had been doing a unit on poetry. I took the book into my lap; it fell open to a poem by Dylan Thomas, "Do Not Go Gentle into That Good Night."

The message of the poem was not to go gentle into death! Fight it! "Rage, rage against the dying of the light!" That was what I wanted Julie to do.

The night she died, I never wanted to read that poem again.

Julie's fourteenth birthday coincided with the start of my senior year. She would have started high school then, riding to school each morning with me.

Being a senior was supposed to be fun; it was supposed to be the best year of my life. It wasn't. I couldn't concentrate on school. My grades started to slip. I didn't care about getting my college applications in on time. Even getting out of bed became hard. My parents were worried and suggested I see a psychologist, but I had already done that when Julie died. I didn't think anyone could help me.

One day as school ended, I gathered my books and headed toward the parking lot. I must have had my head down because I collided with a young woman on her way into the building. Both of us dropped our armfuls of books and started apologizing.

Something made me look up into this woman's eyes. She said, "Are you okay?" in a way I'll never forget. It wasn't as if she was asking me if I was okay because we had bumped into each other. No, she really was asking if I was okay in a bigger way. But I just mumbled something, quickly gathered up my books, and headed for my car.

A few days later, I saw her again. This time, I was in the grocery store. In the cereal aisle, I stopped to pick up some cornflakes. I remembered how Julie loved cornflakes. Just as I was thinking this, a voice said, "Oh, do you like them? They're my favorite!" There she was again!

Lots of people like cornflakes, I reasoned. No big deal. But as I waited in the checkout line, she was suddenly in line behind me.

She talked about how fall was her favorite time of the year, how soon the leaves would be turning colors again. She had a way of speaking that made me listen. She spoke about the beauty in each of the changing seasons and how quickly time flies.

As I paid for my groceries, she said, "Good-bye! I hope I see you again soon!" I did, too.

As the weeks went by, I became more and more depressed. One night as I was preparing for bed, I stopped and looked out the window. I saw a shooting star and made two wishes. One was that Julie was okay wherever she was and not in pain. And the other was that someone would help me find a way out of my pain, too.

The next day, when I woke up, I did not feel the slightest bit rested. That was the only reason I can think of for my actions that day. I walked to school instead of driving. As I stood at the corner waiting for the light to change, I had a terrible thought: If I just stepped out into the street at just that moment . . . all the pain I had been feeling, all the unhappiness, would end. I looked up. A bus was headed my way. I could do it!

Suddenly as if from nowhere, she was there. The nice young woman was standing next to me as if she and I were walking to school together. She placed her hand on my arm and looked at me while she spoke. I don't even remember what she said. But I knew that she was holding on to me, preventing me from taking that step. And she stayed like that until the light changed.

When we crossed the street, she released her hold on me. "I'm Rachel Galloway," she said. "I interviewed for a job teaching English at your high school, but I took one at another school instead. Too bad. I really liked your school but I wanted to teach freshmen and the opening at your school was only to teach juniors."

"Oh," I said. We continued walking in the direction of my school.

Just as we reached the schoolyard, Rachel said, "What are you learning in English? I always like to know if kids actually like anything they are forced to read."

I told her we were doing Romantic and Victorian poetry. It was okay. I didn't have any feeling one way or the other about it.

Rachel stopped and put down her briefcase. She took out a small well-worn book, which she placed carefully in my palm. Then she curled my fingers over it and said, "This is my favorite book of poems; it's by a more modern poet, Dylan Thomas. I especially like the poem on page thirty-two. You borrow it for a while."

The hair on the back of my neck stood straight up.

I held the book in my lap for just a moment before opening it to the most dog-eared page in the book.

> *Do not go gentle into that good night,*
> *Rage, rage against the dying of the light. . . .*

In the margins were Rachel's notes. I read them even as the words grew blurry with my tears. "Not just death, but rage, fight against all despair, all anger, all the loss of men's dreams." In some English class Rachel had taught or taken, she had studied the meaning of this poem, Julie's poem—my poem.

Its message wasn't just for the dying. It was for the living, too. The message was to go on living. To fight to live if necessary, to overcome fear and loss and pain and search out the light, the light of day.

I never saw her again. I asked my principal the name of the young woman they had interviewed for the English teaching position at our school. But he just looked at me kind of funny. "We don't have any openings for English teachers here."

Wherever Julie is, I know she's with a wonderful angel, one who likes poetry and cornflakes, one who brought me a special message, and one who is watching over us all. ✳

*Even though Joanne was my best friend,* I was always a little bit jealous of her. She was beautiful. Wherever we went—school, the mall, movie theaters—Joanne attracted attention. Whenever we were together, I would stand a few feet away from her while the boys talked to her. I was too shy and self-conscious to join in the conversation. Besides, I knew the boys weren't really interested in me, anyway.

By the time we were in high school, the boys wanted to do more than just look at Joanne and talk. Joanne developed the habit of getting into a car with a boy, or a couple of boys, even if she had just met them. After about half an hour, she would return, and we would call my mother to come and pick us up. Joanne and I would wait in silence until my mother arrived.

I never asked Joanne exactly what went on in those cars. I was afraid to know the truth. I couldn't talk about it, not with Joanne or anybody. Part of me knew what the right thing was to do—leave her and go home where it was safe. But a part of me didn't want to miss out on the excitement. Joanne seemed so confident, so brave. When I stood there watching the boys flock around her, I was always tempted to push myself forward, to offer myself up to those boys. But I couldn't. I wasn't Joanne. I watched her get into the cars. Each time, I prayed that she would come back.

When my mother picked us up, she usually assumed that Joanne would sleep over at our house. By the time we were sophomores in high school, Joanne slept over almost every night.

Sometimes, after school, on our way to my house, we would stop by her house quickly so that she could pick up a change of clothing and say hello to her mother. We rarely saw her father, which was just as well. The few times I had met him, he was surly and irritable. I was afraid of him. I always breathed the fresh air deeply when we left Joanne's. The atmosphere inside her house was oppressive. It wasn't just the thick haze of cigarette smoke, either. There was danger there.

One afternoon, when we stopped by, Joanne's two little sisters were sitting on the couch; they had been crying. Joanne's mother peeked around the doorway to the kitchen as we entered, but she didn't come out.

But Joanne's father did. He leaped up from his chair and came charging at us, screaming incoherently. In his hand was a broom handle, which he brought down hard on Joanne's back as she and I ran from the room. Safely behind her locked bedroom door, we panted, waiting for him to go away.

I looked at Joanne. Incredibly, she wasn't crying. She didn't even seem to be upset. "It's nothing," she said. "He only gets like this when he's drunk." Holding up a black skirt and a pink-and-green print blouse, she turned to face me. "Do these go together?" she asked calmly.

The subject was closed. When we were ready to leave, Joanne quietly opened the bedroom door and we slipped across the hall into the kitchen. "Bye, Mom," Joanne said, kissing her mother on her cheek. It was bruised and swollen.

The questions burst out of me. "How can you let him do that? Why doesn't your mother do something?"

Joanne just looked at the ground. "There's nothing anyone can do," she said carefully. "My mom needs him; she doesn't have any money."

"But what about your sisters?" I persisted.

Joanne stopped and looked at me for a moment. "There's nothing anyone can do," she repeated. "Look—my mom doesn't have a job. She doesn't even know how to drive, so she couldn't get to one if she had one. And who would take care of the little kids? Besides, my father doesn't want her working."

I wanted to ask my parents what we should do. But Joanne wouldn't let me tell. "You don't know anything!" she cried angrily. "You think it's so easy to fix. Well, it isn't and nothing will ever be all right. If I told anyone, he would just take it out on me and my mother, and maybe on the little kids, too."

I was silent. What could I do? If I told, it would mean the end of our friendship, and who knew what her father was capable of?

I didn't tell. I prayed for a miracle to change Joanne's life.

As the end of our junior year approached, Joanne was coming to school less and less. We would start out each morning, but often she would turn abruptly at a corner and say, "I'll see you later." She never explained where she was going, but I knew that there were boys. Older boys, sometimes, from the local community college. She went out at night a lot, too. When it got late and she wasn't back, my parents just assumed that she was at her own house. I never told. Joanne dropped out of school at the end of our junior year. She also dropped out of my life. She didn't sleep at my house. I didn't know where she was sleeping, but it was easier not to know. One thing was sure: She was headed toward disaster.

I started my senior year in high school without her. I made new friends and tried not to think about her that much. It was a relief, really. My new friends were so normal. They had families who ate dinner together every night, parents who talked to us, who laughed. I didn't have to worry about being responsible for the safety of these friends, or about what might happen to them when they went home.

One day in May, all of the seniors went to the gym after school for graduation practice. A boy I knew only slightly came up to me. "Hey," he said. He was one of the popular kids, a starter on the football team. I couldn't imagine what he wanted from me.

"You know your friend Joanne?" he said. I braced myself for some terrible recital of her in the backseat of one of his friend's cars.

"What about her?" I asked warily.

"I heard she's in the hospital. My mom's a nurse. She works there. My mom said Joanne tried to kill herself. I just thought you should know."

How could I have let this happen? I felt terribly guilty and ashamed.

The minute I walked in the door at home and saw my mother, I burst into tears. The whole story came pouring out of me. My mother held me until I was able to stop crying. Then she said, "Let's go."

Joanne was in a coma. She was lying very still in the bed, her skin white and taut. I could see her bones protruding from her shrunken body and every vein stood out blue against her white skin. She looked like a skeleton, like someone who was already dead.

She had tried to starve herself.

I looked at my friend. Was this the girl I had been jealous of? I reached out and took her hand. "Oh, Joanne, come back, please come back. Don't die. Everything will be okay, you'll see. Just come back!"

I visited Joanne every day that week, but there was no change. I got to know the nurses well and they advised me not to expect too much. I guess they wanted to prepare me for the worst.

Incredibly, it didn't happen. When we got the call that told us that Joanne had opened her eyes, we flew to the hospital. I ran down the hallway to Joanne's room, but I stopped just outside the door. I was almost afraid to look. I took a deep breath and pushed the door open. Joanne looked up as I entered the room. She smiled. "I knew you'd come," she said.

Joanne told me about her pain and fear and loneliness.

She told me she wanted to escape it all. And the only way she knew how to do that was to die.

"But then I changed my mind. Or rather, someone changed it for me. I think I was close to being dead because I saw a light. Only I couldn't get to it. An angel kept telling me I had to come back." She laughed. "I guess all those years of Sunday school paid off, because I knew I couldn't say no to an angel."

The doctors told us that Joanne had probably heard my voice through her coma, telling her to come back.

Those of us who know her know that she was telling the truth. Because even I couldn't work the miracle that happened after Joanne got out of the hospital. Her suicide attempt brought the attention of people who could help. Her father started going to AA. More important, he *continued* going to AA. The whole family went for counseling. Eventually, Joanne finished high school and got married. Her son is two years old.

If anyone deserved a miracle, Joanne did, God knows. And He gave her one. ✴

*I* never felt attractive. I always wanted to lose ten pounds. Even though my mother and my friends told me I was fine the way I was, those ten pounds, I imagined, would make all the difference in my life.

At the beginning of my sophomore year in high school, I determined to do something about it. I knew that some of the older girls—seniors—dieted really strictly. I watched them whip out their lunches of diet sodas and apples. But I was hungry at lunch time and again at three in the afternoon no matter what I ate. I just couldn't starve myself.

When I complained to my friend, Jean, she told me that her sister had something. She opened her purse and took out a few tiny red pills, and she pressed them into my hand. "Appetite suppressants," Jean said. "They'll help you forget you're hungry!" She was right. I lost a few pounds.

But then I needed more pills to keep the weight off.

That's how it began. I loved those little red pills—amphetamines. I didn't care that they were addictive, that I was an addict. I worked two jobs and could afford to spend my money on them. I loved that they put me in control of my appetite. And they gave me so much energy. If I had trouble sleeping or sitting still in class, I ignored it. I even ignored the posters that were all around my high school warning kids that amphetamines can raise your heart rate and even kill you. Nothing could hurt me. I was sixteen and I would live forever.

My parents noticed the change in me. They began to bug me about my weight loss, but nothing would make me give up my pills. I hid them. I never left them in my room when I wasn't there. I was afraid that my mother or my nosy little brother would come snooping and find them.

I kept my pills in a red case in my purse. I was very careful to check to make sure that I had them with me at all times. The case also had my wallet with my driver's license, student ID, and all my money. I guarded it with my life.

When my parents announced that they had made plans for me for the first half of summer vacation, I was flabbergasted. How dare they? I wanted to hang out with my friends, go to the beach and the mall and just relax. I was so angry, I didn't even want to hear where they were sending me. No matter where it was, I wouldn't go.

I didn't have a choice. Before I knew what was happening, we had shopped, packed, and bought the ticket.

I was on my way to Flagstaff, Arizona, to a summer camp. But it wasn't just any kind of camp. Daily activities included hiking up the mountains, early morning runs, yoga and aerobics and special classes in learning to make good choices. It sounded like torture. It was rehab.

At the airport, I didn't even kiss my parents good-bye. They could make me go but they couldn't make me enjoy it. I checked my purse for my red case. My pills were there. I hoped I had enough to last the month. What would I do if I ran out?

I looked at my ticket and went to find my seat—22A. I took off my coat and put it and my purse in the overhead compartment. Then I fastened my seat belt and plugged in my headset. For the next four hours, I tried to make myself oblivious to everything around me.

When the plane landed, I collected my coat and my purse and headed off the plane. A very tan girl in shorts met me at the gate. She introduced herself to me as Jodi and we went to get my bags. Then we boarded a small bus where ten or twelve other girls were already waiting.

Out of habit, I opened my purse to check on my case. It was gone!

I was near hysterics. But Jodi said calmly, "We'll make a claim from camp. If it's still on the plane, someone will find it."

What was I going to do? I knew I'd gain weight in four weeks without my pills.

I cried myself to sleep the first night. It was the last time I had any time to myself.

After the first day, which included a three-mile hike straight up a mountain and two aerobics and swim classes, every part of me hurt. I felt like I was in boot camp.

By the second day, I was throwing up. The staff gave me some good-tasting tea to drink and some cold packs for my head. Jodi talked to me a lot and told me that when she first started coming here, she didn't even make it through the first day without throwing up.

If I had known anything at all at the time, I would have recognized in myself the symptoms of drug withdrawal. But I was too sore and too upset to even think about my pills. When I asked if the airline had found my wallet, Jodi said no, they had looked all over the plane but they didn't find it.

I fell into bed at night too exhausted to think. So did most of the other girls. It was only at mealtimes that we talked to each other. Jennifer and Marcy came from New York. Elizabeth was from San Francisco, Jessica was from Los Angeles, and Tricia was from Portland, Oregon. All of us had been forced to come to camp because we had an addiction—diet pills, alcohol, or pot.

With each passing day, my body was getting stronger. By the end of the second week, I was amazed. I had no trouble waking up at five A.M. for a freezing cold swim in the lake. Three-mile hikes became ten-mile hikes. And getting across the ropes course blindfolded was a breeze.

At mealtimes, I was ravenous. Without my pills, I thought for sure I would gain weight. But with all the exercise, I found that my jeans and shorts were actually getting loose on me. I didn't need a scale to tell me that I was looking great.

I felt great! By the end of the four weeks, I didn't miss those pills and I had a great tan, some new muscles, and a few new friends. We promised to keep in touch during the school year.

As I boarded the plane, I remembered my missing case. Oh well, I thought, it's gone. Strangely, I wasn't so upset anymore.

I moved toward my seat. That's when I realized that I had been given exactly the same seat assignment going home as I had on the way out. Not too unusual, I thought. But maybe . . . Should I look in the overhead bin just to make sure? It was impossible. It probably wasn't the same plane. And even if by some remote chance it was the same plane, the crew had searched it thoroughly.

It was right there in the overhead compartment of seat 22A.

Everything was exactly as I had left it. I sat down in my seat and clutched the case, trying to decide what I felt. That's when it hit me.

I felt great! Physically and emotionally terrific! I had worked hard to make myself feel and look this way and I had done it myself without the pills.

But I knew I hadn't done it alone. Some higher power had made me reach inside myself and find out what I was truly capable of. Some higher power had hidden those pills from me for a month so that I would see that I didn't really need them.

But why had I found them again?

I knew the answer. It had to be my decision to use or not, no one else's.

I waited for the plane to take off, for the seat belt sign to be turned off, for the lavatory to be unoccupied. Then I entered the little cubicle, opened the toilet, emptied out my bright red case, and watched all those bright red pills get flushed.

The high I felt had nothing to do with the plane's altitude. ⸓

*When people find out I come from a* family with seven children, I hear things like, "Do you have to grab food at the table to be sure you get any?" or "How do your parents remember all your names?" or "How do you ever get your mom's attention?" But growing up in a large close-knit family is wonderful. I am the baby and I've never lacked for attention. If my mother or father wasn't available to give it, one of my siblings always was.

Being number seven meant that I became an aunt at fifteen. This made me very cool to my friends. I'm sure I will always love all my nieces and nephews, but the child of my oldest brother, John, and his wife, Mary, will always have a special place in my heart.

Just after Mary found out she was pregnant, my brother John started having stomach pains. For a while, we all teased him, telling him that he was having a sympathetic pregnancy. But as Mary approached the end of her first trimester and her morning sickness stopped, John became progressively worse. After a lot of tests, doctors gave us all terrible news: John had colon cancer. He was only twenty-six years old.

I was in eleventh grade and I couldn't believe that this was happening. We had always been a religious family, but now I asked why God would do such a thing. John was such a good person. And we all needed him so much. Not just me, but our parents and especially Mary and the new baby.

John had surgery, then chemotherapy and radiation. His cancer didn't respond and it became a waiting game to see whether or not he would live to see his child.

In Mary's twentieth week, she had an ultrasound test, and they came to our house to tell us they were having a boy. Then they told us the baby would be named John.

When I heard that they were going to name the baby after my brother, I thought, Oh, no! That will mean that John will die! The words "The Lord giveth and the Lord taketh" from the Bible ran through my mind. It terrified me and I ran to my room, slammed the door, and cried.

Then I had an odd thought. Suppose they chose another name for this baby? Suppose they named him Christopher or Patrick or Luke or any one of a thousand names that just weren't the one my brother had? John was still here. The thought of giving his name to the baby made me feel as if my brother and his wife had given up hope. They were creating a new little John to replace my brother. I knew I wasn't being rational at all but I didn't care. It became an obsession with me. If I could just get them to consider a different name for the baby, maybe God wouldn't take my brother.

I began to suggest different names whenever I saw my brother or Mary. I couldn't tell them why I wanted them to choose another name but they never asked anyway. Mary would just kind of smile and nod at me when I brought up the subject.

It was a terrible time, those months of Mary's pregnancy and John's treatment. I couldn't think straight. I had trouble sleeping and I started doing poorly in school. I knew we were supposed to be happy about the baby, that a new life was a reason for hope and joy. But I didn't feel hopeful and I couldn't feel joy. I watched my brother get weaker and thinner each day and I became angrier and angrier.

The problem was, I didn't know who I was angry at. God? The new baby? John? Mary? All of them?

One month before Mary's due date, my brother John entered the hospital for the last time. We knew that the doctors would have to put a tube down his throat to keep him nourished because he couldn't eat or drink anything. Before they did that, John wanted to speak to each of us. I'll never know what he said to my parents or to my other brothers and sisters but I'll always remember the words he said to me.

He told me to look for him in his son's eyes.

I know John wanted to comfort me but this was not the comfort I wanted. Why did he have to die? Why did the baby get to be here but not my brother? It wasn't fair! And then I had the most horrible thought: If God had to take one of them, why couldn't he take the baby and not John?

Nothing will ever make me believe that God didn't hear my prayer, because a day later my sister-in-law began having complications. The baby wasn't due for several weeks but he stopped moving. Mary was rushed to the hospital where doctors performed a cesarean section. Our entire family waited outside the operating room for word about both of them. As I looked at the stricken faces of my parents, siblings, and of Mary's parents, I kept thinking that this was all my fault. How would I face them if anything happened to the baby or, worse yet, to Mary?

In the waiting room was a little desk with some paper and pencils on it. I sat down at the desk, thinking I would write a note to everybody—to my brother and sister-in-law, my parents, everyone—and beg them all to forgive me. If anything happened to this baby, how could I live with myself? But try as I might, I couldn't write one word. I just couldn't.

I'll never know what made me do what I did next, but I opened the drawer of the desk. Inside was a Bible. I opened it. The first passage that caught my eye came from Matthew 28:20: "Lo, I am with you always, even unto the end of the world."

An hour later, the door to the waiting room opened and a smiling doctor in blue scrubs came out. "Everything is fine," he said. "The baby was small—under five pounds—but what a fighter! He was crying before we even got him all the way out—a very good sign." Everyone crowded around the doctor, asking questions. Mary's parents were the first allowed in to see her. My parents hugged each other. No one except me seemed to notice that John wasn't there celebrating this birth with us. He was lying upstairs in another part of the hospital with tubes attached to him. Was he still with us?

He was. And he lived to see his son. Two days later, Mary

and the baby were wheeled into John's room where he held his son briefly. I wasn't there to see the expression on my brother's face, but Mary told me later that peace was written all over his face. He died that night.

My nephew was strong and healthy. After only a week, he and Mary were allowed to go home. My parents and I helped gather up all the flowers in Mary's room. While we were preparing to leave, a nurse came in to ask Mary to sign the baby's birth certificate. She did, but then my sister-in-law handed the certificate to me. She said, "Your brother asked me to show you this."

I looked at the document with my nephew's vital data— date and time of birth and his name. I had assumed that the baby would be named John. He was, but John was his middle name. Mary and my brother-in-heaven had named my nephew, Matthew.

About a week later, I woke up in the middle of the night. My room was warm but I had an odd sensation. Something had nagged at me since Matthew's birth, since I had seen that birth certificate. Suddenly I knew exactly what it was. I switched on my light and looked in my Bible. I turned to John. Matthew had been born at 2:18 A.M., but hospitals record time like they do in the military. Two eighteen was fourteen eighteen. And there it was, my brother's message loud and clear: John 14:18: "I will not leave you comfortless."

Out of all his aunts and uncles and grandparents, I'm his favorite babysitter, and everyone agrees Matthew really does have his father's eyes!

*My father worked for a company that* began laying off people after 9/11. Though he knew it was only a matter of time before they axed him, too, he was really shocked when it happened. I guess he just never really believed that after thirty years, he would find himself out of a job.

He tried looking for a new job, but nobody wanted to hire a fifty-two-year-old man—even one with lots of experience.

It was really hard to be around him after awhile. He got very depressed and was angry almost all the time. Nothing was fun with him anymore. We used to go to ball games or at least watch them together on TV. But my dad didn't want to do anything like that anymore. After awhile, he didn't want to do much of anything.

My mother said he was depressed, that he had lost his sense of purpose and self-esteem. He was used to being the provider, the breadwinner in our family.

I was worried about him. If my mom put some music on and asked him to dance with her, he said no and went into another room and shut the door—I guess to shut out the music but maybe to shut out us, too. If my sister asked him to help her with her homework, he just said no and told me to do it.

And if I asked him just to have a game of catch with me in

the backyard, he told me he was too tired, that we'd play another time. As the end of school approached, I looked for a summer job. I wanted to be out of the house. I just couldn't stand to see my dad sit, day after day, in his old leather chair in the den, staring at nothing.

One day as I was getting ready to leave for my job at the grocery store, an elderly lady I vaguely recognized who lived down the street called out to me.

"Can you help me a minute, son?" she asked. She told me that her garage door wouldn't work and she had to get her car out. I didn't know anything about garage doors but I told her I'd go inside and ask my dad if he could help her.

"Your dad?" she asked. "Is he home? Oh, great!" When I got home later that day, my dad told me that he had fixed Mrs. Linden's garage door.

The next day I saw Mrs. Linden outside again as I left for work. "Why is your dad home during the day?" she asked. I wasn't sure I should tell her because being out of work seemed like a bad thing—I know my dad was pretty ashamed. But Mrs. Linden seemed genuinely interested. So I told her. Then I had a terrible thought! Suppose Mrs. Linden should offer to pay my dad for helping her! He would be so ashamed! "Please don't tell him I told you . . ." I began, but Mrs. Linden put her hand on my arm. "Don't worry. My son-in-law got laid off, too. There's no shame in it but it does take a toll on a man, doesn't it? My son-in-law is proud, too. He won't let me help them. And I suppose your dad won't take anything for helping me, either, would he?" I shook my head. "Well, then, I'll just bake him some cookies." She turned away and I went to work thinking what a nice lady she was.

A couple of days later, Mrs. Linden rang our bell. She asked for my dad. "Paul, would you mind taking a look at my washing machine? I know it's a lot to ask, but it has been making funny noises and I can't really afford to have a repair-man out . . ."

My dad was over there a long time.

"Do you think it's a lot of nerve for Mrs. Linden to come and ask favors from Dad?" I asked my mom. She looked surprised. "Why, no, I think it's wonderful! Just look at your father's face when he gets back."

My mother was right. When my dad came home much later, he looked tired but for the first time in a long while, he really talked to us.

"I took that whole machine apart and put it back together! It took me hours. I've never had to do anything like that but I guess if you want to know how a thing works, you have to take it apart to see what's inside it."

He was even humming a little as he put his tools away.

The next morning, my dad was out before I got up. What was going on?

He came back around noon with a big grin on his face. "I got a job! I asked Ben at the hardware store if he knew any of the people in the appliance repair business. He put me in touch with an old guy who fixes all kinds of things. He agreed to take me on as an apprentice. I won't make much at first. But I'll learn the business and from what I understand, there's more than enough work out there."

Here was my dad who had worked his whole life as an executive in an office. He wore a suit to work and traveled. Now he was talking about wearing a workman's tool belt and getting his hands dirty! And he was excited about it! Well, it was okay with me if it meant that he got out of the house every day and came home with a smile.

"Come on son, let's go have a catch in the backyard! I'll tell you all about what the inside of a dishwasher looks like!"

Several weeks went by and the change in my dad was amazing. He told me that fixing things was like solving a puzzle. You had to use your brains to figure out what was wrong and then you had to fix it so it wouldn't break again. And you had to do all this while learning about electricity and the wire placement and a whole bunch of other stuff. I loved just watching his face when he talked about it. It was nice to have my old dad back!

One day as I passed Mrs. Linden's house, I saw her sitting outside. She didn't look too well. She told me she was just a little under the weather. She said she felt a lot better outside.

I told her that my dad had gotten a job as an appliance repairman and that we owed it all to her. "He really is good at fixing things," she said. "You know besides my garage door and washing machine, he got all my electrical gadgets—my doorbell, my dishwasher, and my garbage disposal—working right. It's been so long since I've been able to use most of my appliances because when they broke down, I couldn't afford to have anyone out to fix them.

"I could tell that your dad liked fixing things, seeing something that wasn't any use to anybody suddenly become useful again. I guess the same is true of people."

When I got home, I told my mom I'd seen Mrs. Linden and that she didn't feel well. My mom said she would go over there later in the day to check on her.

At dinner, my mom complained of a terrible headache. She had been visiting Mrs. Linden, who also had a headache and was feeling sick to her stomach. "I hope I didn't catch a virus from her or anything like that," my mom said. "Anyway, I'm feeling better since I left her house. I guess it was the power of suggestion—if you're around someone who isn't well, you start feeling that way yourself."

My dad stared at my mother. Then all of a sudden, he jumped up from the table and ran out of the house. I followed him to Mrs. Linden's house.

"Carbon monoxide," my dad explained on the way to the hospital with Mrs. Linden and my mom, "builds up. It doesn't have any smell or anything and it can kill you. Luckily Mrs. Linden kept going outside when she was feeling ill."

Mrs. Linden had forgotten to put a new battery in her carbon monoxide detector. She had a lot of carbon monoxide in her blood. She would have to stay in the hospital for a while. My mother just had a trace amount and was allowed to go home after a few hours.

When Mrs. Linden left the hospital, she came to stay with us while her house was aired out.

After a week, her daughter and son-in-law came to visit her. They came over to thank my dad.

"No need for thanks," he said. He told them that he never would have thought about trying to work as a repairman if Mrs. Linden hadn't needed him to try to fix her appliances. She really worked a miracle for him. Her daughter said my father had more than returned the favor.

As they left, Mrs. Linden's son-in-law turned to my parents and said, "We also want to thank you for allowing my mother-in-law to stay here this past week. We just couldn't get away before this—since I've started my new job!" He seemed really happy. "Thanks for having Hope!" For just a minute, my parents looked surprised, but then we all realized that "Hope" was Mrs. Linden's first name!

I knew my dad was really addressing God when he said, softly, "Thanks for giving me a reason to."

*I*'ve lived my whole life in a wheelchair because I was born with spina bifida, and I don't consider myself an invalid. Nor does anyone in my family or circle of friends. The reason for this is that I can do almost everything that anyone else can do, including playing sports and driving a car. The only thing I can't do is walk, but I still believe that that will change someday.

I've played in several wheelchair Olympics and my wheelchair basketball team has always won. Basketball is one of my passions. Another one of my passions is a girl named Bethany Mills.

We started dating around Halloween. I took her to the movies and out to eat afterward. I don't remember one time on that date where either of us referred in any way to my being in a wheelchair. We were too busy getting to know each other.

Since then, as we've gotten closer, the subject has come up, but only in terms of how we have to make allowances for it. She says she doesn't mind sitting on my lap to make out, and she's gotten used to seeing me drive my car with the hand pedals.

Our high school is located in the middle of New York City and is very large. The building is old but was renovated several years ago to make it handicap accessible. Now, there are plenty of ramps and an elevator. I'm always the first one to class because of that elevator. All my friends have to take the crowded stairs; they aren't allowed to ride with me.

I've always been grateful for all the things I can do. About the only thing I could think of that my friends could do, be, or look forward to in their lives that I couldn't is their ability to get into professions where they could help others. Since September 11, a lot of the kids in my group have been talking about becoming firefighters or police officers. Suddenly, the public saw how truly heroic people who go into those professions have to be. I know that some of my friends will probably go into those fields, but I just assumed that those would be two areas that would be off-limits to a guy in a wheelchair.

Then something happened that made me believe that anything is possible.

In April, Bethany and I tried out for the school play and I got the part of Mercutio, one of Romeo's friends who has this great fight scene. Bethany got the role of the nurse. We practiced after school in the English room with the drama teacher, Miss Barry.

Miss Barry had no trouble staging a fight scene around a guy in a wheelchair and everyone was very excited about the whole production. There were about ten cast members and Miss Barry practicing after school on a warm April day when, suddenly, the power went out!

Now we've all lived through New York power outages. They usually happen in the hottest part of the summer when everyone has air conditioners on, but this was only April, so we assumed the power was down only at our school. But when Bethany looked out the window, she saw that the power was down as far as she could see. She was looking west toward the Hudson River.

Miss Barry told everyone to stay calm and wait to see if the lights would come back on. After about five minutes though, she decided that we should leave. That's when we realized that I couldn't get out. The elevator was, of course, useless, and there weren't enough guys left in the building to carry me down three flights of stairs to the street level.

With no air conditioning, the classroom was getting very stuffy even with the windows open. Miss Barry called the fire department and explained our situation. They promised to send a truck.

It was really the first time I ever felt like an inconvenience. I told Miss Barry to go on home. Bethany would wait with me until the firemen could get me down the stairs. Miss Barry looked at me for a minute; then she told Bethany to come downstairs and wait at the front door so she could direct the firemen when they arrived. It would be only a minute or two.

They left and I wheeled over to the window to watch the action on the street.

For some reason, something, a flash of light maybe, caught my eye. I looked west, as Bethany had done just a few seconds ago. Peering between the tall buildings, I swept my gaze as far as I could but I didn't see anything unusual. I felt weird, uneasy.

I assumed I must be feeling that way because, even though I wasn't in any danger, I was so helpless just waiting there for someone to carry me down to the street level. But . . . there it was again! A little flash of light from somewhere. But from where? And again, the flash wasn't in my direct line of vision; it was only a little perception somewhere in my peripheral vision field. It was annoying.

I turned around and began reading all the posters on the wall of the English room. My gaze rested on a poster of the blind poet Milton. Underneath his picture (which had never held the slightest bit of interest for me before) was a line from one of his poems: "They also serve who only stand and wait."

Well, I was getting tired of waiting all right! Where were those firemen? I began to wish that Bethany would come back up and keep me company. I decided to call out the window to see if I could attract someone's attention.

That's when I saw him! He couldn't have been more than four years old and he was out on the roof of an apartment building some blocks away from where I was. I watched him for a minute. He walked back and forth from the edge of the building, which had no ledge, to a big metal door. He pulled on the handle of the door with all his might. I could see his little body pulling back and forth, both hands clasping the door handle. But either the door was too heavy or it must have locked from the inside. That little boy was trapped.

I was afraid to glance away from him for a second. He hadn't been easy to spot among all the rest of the buildings between him and me. Even when I heard Bethany's voice and the firemen coming up the stairs, I didn't turn around.

"Help him!" I pointed when they came into the classroom. "Help who?" The firemen looked out the window. "There, right there, he's on the roof of a building. Can't you see?" And then I realized why they couldn't see the little boy but I could—the firefighters were standing and I was sitting. The boy was directly in my line of vision! I pulled at the sleeve of the firefighter, who, crouching down, saw him almost immediately. He punched the radio on his shoulder and spoke into it.

Then he turned to me. "Don't worry. Emergency teams are responding. They'll get him. Now let's just get you downstairs." It took two of them to carry me and my wheelchair down the three flights to the ground level.

Outside, I took a few big gulps of air. The air felt heavy, like rain.

Before I got into my car, one of them came over to tell me, "They got him! Babysitter fell asleep and he went up on the roof for some air. The door slammed shut behind him. It wasn't even locked, just too heavy for the kid to open. He's only four years old!

"You know, son. It was amazing that you saw that kid. He was six blocks away, too high up for anyone to hear him call, and he didn't have any way to attract anyone's attention. There's probably a mayor's thank-you coming your way. Fact is, he was in your line of sight. No one else would have noticed him. You had to have been sitting to see him! Good work, kid."

I breathed again. Suddenly, the air didn't feel so heavy anymore.

On Monday, everyone in school knew what had happened. But in English class, I looked at that Milton poster again. I understood what it meant. *"They also serve who only stand and wait."* You don't have to be the guy who runs into the burning building to save a life. You can also help someone just by being aware when there is a need. You can use the talents and capabilities you do have—sometimes they are all that's needed.

I had served, even though I'd been sitting and waiting, not standing and waiting.

Our production of *Romeo and Juliet* was a sellout. I got a standing ovation but I knew it wasn't for the role I had played on stage. It was for the role I had played in Miss Barry's English classroom during the April power outage—the role someone knew I was meant to play!

# Attention All Teens!

*If* you enjoyed the stories in this book and you think you have one to share, *Teen Miracles* is waiting to hear from you! Have you felt the hand of God or some higher power in your life? Have you felt part of an amazing circumstance that touched you in a way you can't explain? Have you ever felt truly blessed? Do you have a story you think will inspire others or offer hope? Have you experienced a miracle?

If so, we want to hear from you!

The stories in this book are intended to offer inspiration that we are all capable of reaching our highest potential. You, too, can be part of this process.

Send your stories for consideration for future collections to *storysubmissions@adamsmedia.com*. Your story could touch someone who needs it!